中級 英語の世間話

第4版

Peter Burden

Small talk in the Classroom

大学教育出版

HOW TO USE THE TEXTBOOK

The book is divided into nine units, with each unit designed to last at least two sixty minutes classes. Each unit starts with a dialogue which introduces much of the vocabulary and new words that will appear in subsequent exercises and freer conversation practice as the unit progresses. The model conversation is based on the exploits of Bill and Yuko. Bill is British and is an exchange student at a Japanese university and meets Yuko on the first day of the new school year. On one level, the two characters are one dimensional conversation practice, but it is possible to see a progression in their relationship that will hopefully interest the learners.

1. Model Dialogues
Prior to reading, the students should try to find the answers to introductory background questions. Subsequently, the conversations should be read with a partner. The conversations have relevant contexts and use of language so giving learners practice in grammar, vocabulary, and appropriate style and conversation strategies when communication inevitably breaks down. If possible, the students should 'read and look up' and just read the dialogues word for word. They should scan the line, and then look at their conversation partner. In order to make the conversations more natural, the teacher should model both halves with different students highlighting gesture and intonation.

2. Questionnaires
Each unit has a questionnaire which expands on vocabulary. Again, the use is up to the classroom teacher, but one way is to ask a student to read question 1 aloud, then another student read 2 and so on. Then, in turns, the students can read aloud with the person sitting next to them and be encouraged to seek clarification. Students can then silently complete the questionnaire and then come back together as a group and with a show of hands express their opinions, as students are often interested in each other's viewpoints. Alternatively, the students can incorporate the question or statement with their chosen response to give an opinion, which is shared with their partner who is encouraged to contribute by using "How about you?" The students can then be encouraged to continue the conversations using any language knowledge they possess.

3. Practice Dialogues

The students fill in the blanks matching the number with an appropriate example. Repetition allows for heuristic understanding as well as requiring the learners to listen carefully so that an appropriate word is used. Realizing that vocabulary should be effectively taught in the context within which it is being practiced, guessing and predicting meaning is important. Lastly, the students should be allowed to supply their own information from their own experience.

4. Pair work and 'Jigsaw' type activities

These allow for further freer practice and again the uses of strategies to help prevent conversational breakdowns can be drawn attention to. Also, as in real time conversation, there is a chance to build on the conversation to allow for more than QA QA QA type interactions.

5. What percent of people...?

In the book there are occasional pages with interesting facts about Japan. This should give students practice in describing frequencies and percentages. At first there is usually an information gap exercise so that students pay close attention to detail. It is important in these exercises that the teacher models the questions. After reading the data, the students ask the questions underneath, and then make similar questions based on the data they read. After that, students should practice asking their partners or other students how often they do something. Again, the teacher could model questioning and answering if the students are still not confident.

6. Tables and Charts

In the unit are reading tasks involving authentic data related to the theme of the unit. This is to focus interest in the theme and allows for a wider understanding of the context and relevance of the topic. Activities should allow for practice in interpreting data, reading large numbers, surmising information from data and asking relevant questions based on the information in front of them.

7. Finding things in common exercises

This practice is perhaps the most important part of the unit as it checks understanding while allowing for student generated interaction. The practice usually begins with the students asking questions to the teacher on a theme such as "childhood memories" or "tastes in movies." The teacher's responses are noted in the table. Then the students fill in their own answers and have to think of additional questions. After the teacher has checked a few students' answers, the students are free to walk around the room and ask two or three of their classmates. They should not talk to the person sitting next to them in the classroom. After asking for the family name, the students should take notes of the other student's replies. Subsequently, the students are asked to look at the answers to the questions, find commonalities and to make sentences. The teacher will need to demonstrate how to write these sentences in the first instance.

8. Snapshots

Here there are three chances to read some information about life in Bill's home country, Britain. Although the vocabulary may be difficult as this is a chance to read natural information, it gives the students chances to read about life in Britain that may interest the students as they show differences between customs and culture in Britain and in Japan, or their country. While it is up to the teacher and the students to decide how to engage with this material, it may be possible for the students to ask each other about difficult words to clarify meaning and to contrast the information with the student's own lifestyle.

9. Find someone who...?

These exercises are introduced a number of times and provide final practice. The students walk around the room to ask questions and fill in the left hand side with the family names of students who have responded 'yes' to the question. Preferably, each question should have a different family name, although this may be difficult when class sizes are small.

授業で役に立つ表現
Useful Phrases for the Classroom

①すみません、わかりません。
I'm sorry I don't understand.

②もう一度言っていただけませんか。
Could you repeat that, please?/Once more, please.

③もう少しゆっくり話してください。
Could you speak more slowly, please?

④すみません、知りません。
I'm sorry I don't know.

⑤_____とはどういう意味ですか。
What does _____ mean?

⑥_____のスペルを教えてください。
Could you spell _____, please?

⑦_____は英語で何と言うのですか。
How do you say _____ in English?

⑧もう少し簡単な英語で説明できますか。
Can you explain in simpler English?

⑨他の言い方で言っていただけますか。
Could you say it in other words?

⑩すみません、聞き取れません。
Sorry, I can't catch your words.

⑪私の言うことがわかりますか。
Do you understand what I'm saying?

⑫適当な言葉が見つかりません。
I can't find the proper words.

From now on, there is very little Japanese language in the book. Of course you can use Japanese if you want or have to, but try to use the above expressions when you do not understand.

Contents

Find someone who...?

As this is the first class, it is useful to find some things in common with your classmates. This is an "ice-breaker" game. Walk around the room and ask questions. If someone says "Yes", write the family name AND a follow-up question using a Wh- question.

1. _____ thinks this will be an easy class.

2. _____ has seen a movie at a movie theater recently.

3. _____ has a birthday in April.

4. _____ can swim more than two kilometers.

5. _____ really likes learning English.

6. _____ has gone to *karaoke* recently.

7. _____ can remember the teacher's family name.

8. _____ likes cycling in his/her free time.

9. _____ has been to two foreign countries.

10. _____ can remember where the teacher's hometown is.

11. _____ has more than 5 foreign friends on Facebook.

12. _____ wants to try bungee jumping in New Zealand.

13. _____ enjoys eating natto for breakfast.

14. _____ has an interesting part time job.

15. _____ wants to go to Europe someday.

16. _____ believes there is life on another planet.

17. _____ enjoys listening to British rock music.

18. _____ has been to Hokkaido or Okinawa.

19. _____ is scared of high buildings.

20. _____ knows who Neil Armstrong is.

21. _____ _____

UNIT 1

Meeting someone for the first time

Here is a conversation between Bill and Yuko. They are meeting for the first time.

Before you read with a partner, find the answers to these questions:

1) *Where does Yuko live now? Why?*
2) *Where's Bill from?*
3) *What's Bill's hometown like?*
4) *What is Yuko's major?*

Now read the conversation with your partner.

1 Bill: Hello, nice to meet you. I'm Bill Anderson.

Yuko: Hi, good to meet you too. I'm Yuko Yamashita.

2 Bill: Sorry, I didn't catch your family name. . .

Yuko: It's Yamashita. Spelt Y-A-M-A-S-H-I-T-A.

3 Bill: Ah, Yamashita. I understand now. And where are you from, Yuko?

Yuko: My hometown is Matsuyama in Ehime Prefecture, but now I live in Okayama, as Matsuyama is a long way to commute. How about you?

4 Bill: I'm British. I'm from Bath.

Yuko: Sorry, could you say that again?

5 Bill: Bath. It's a small city in England. It's famous though, as it is an old Roman town. It has a hot spring in the center of town that many tourists like to visit in summer.

Yuko: That's a coincidence! Matsuyama is famous for its hot springs too. By the way, what do you do?

6 Bill: I'm a student. I'm studying Japanese language and I have a part time job working evenings in a convenience store. How about you?

Yuko: I'm a student too. I'm majoring in Law. I don't have a part time job yet. I guess I'm a little too busy doing circle activities. But I'd like one. Maybe later.

7 Bill: What kind of part time job would you like?

Yuko: Well, I don't really know. If I have the chance, I want to work with people. Maybe in a restaurant or supermarket. Perhaps working on weekends.

8 Bill: Well, I've got to run. My class is starting. Hope to see you around, sometime soon.

Yuko: Yeah. Catch you later.

How about you?

1. Do you have a part time job now?
2. What kind of part time job would you like in the future?
3. Are you busy doing club or circle activities?
4. What is your college major?
5. How long does it take you to commute to school?
6. Do you have anything in common with Bill or Yuko?

Listen. Fill in the table about your teacher:

First name	
Family name	
Hometown	
Special ability	
Interests	a) b)
Free time activities	a) b)
Dislikes	a) b)
Favorite music	
Ambition	
Tourist destination	
Strong points of character	a) b)
Weak points of character	a) b)

Umm. That's a tricky question!

I'm not particularly good at anything!. But maybe…

Ambition? I don't know yet, but maybe…

Now, fill in the table about you:

First name	
Family name	
Hometown	
Special ability	
Interests	a) b)
Free time activities	a) b)
Dislikes	a) b)
Favorite music	
Ambition	
Tourist destination	
Strong points of character	a) b)
Weak points of character	a) b)

Look at your answers and your teacher's answers. What do you have in common with the teacher? What differences do you have?

1. The teacher and I both _____ .
2. The teacher and I both _____ .
3. The teacher and I both _____ .
4. _____ .

5. The teacher _____ but I _____ .
6. The teacher _____ but I _____ .
7. The teacher _____ but I _____ .
8. The teacher _____ but I _____ .

Introductions: Nice to meet you/Nice talking to you.

You are meeting your partner for the first time. Practice introducing yourself.

A: Hello, nice to meet you. I'm _____.

B: Hi, good to meet you too. I'm _____.

A: **Sorry, I didn't catch your family name. . .**

B: It's _____. Spelt _____.

A: Ah, _____. I understand now. And where are you from?

B: My hometown is _____ in _____ Prefecture. How about you?

A: I come from _____. By the way, what are you majoring in?

B: **Sorry, I don't understand. What does 'major' mean?**

A: Well, it means 'the subject you are studying at university.'

B: Oh, I see. I'm majoring in _____. How about you?

A: (That's a coincidence I'm in the _____ department, too!)

   (I'm majoring in _____.)

B: Are you enjoying your studies?

A: Yes, they're _____ !

B: Are you doing a part time job, too?

A: (No, not yet. But I would like to work in a _____. How about you?)

   (Yes, I have a part time job in a _____. How about you?)

B: (Me neither. But I'd like to work in a _____.)

   (Me too. I have a part time job in a _____.)

   (Oh, I do. I'm working in a _____.)

   (Yes, me too. I'm working in a _____.)

   (Oh, I don't. But I'd like to work in a _____.)

A: That's interesting. Well, my class is starting. Hope to see you around school, later.

B: OK. Nice talking to you. Catch you later.

Use these words:

   A: Hope _____.

   B: Yeah. Catch _____ .

Ask your partner

Here are many questions. Choose about TEN that look interesting to you.

Ask and answer questions. When you answer, say "How about you?" or

"What do you think?"

How about you?

Ask your partner...	Ask your partner...	Ask your partner...	Ask your partner···
Where do you live now? Answer:	Did you do any club activities in high school? Answer:	What were you good at in junior high school? Answer:	What do you usually like doing at the weekend? Answer:
When are you happiest? Answer:	What is one of your good points of character? Answer:	What is one of your weak points of character? Answer:	Have you ever been to a foreign country? Answer:
What is the most expensive thing you have ever bought? Answer:	What is your favorite place to eat out with your friends? Answer:	What kind of TV programs do you really like? Answer:	What are you scared of? Answer:
What was your best friend in high school like? Answer:	What kinds of movies are you not keen on watching? Answer:	What is something you would really like to do in the future? Answer:	What do you like best about this university? Answer:
What annoys or irritates you? Answer:	What bad habit do you have? Answer:	What is your happiest memory of junior high school? Answer:	Do you have a favorite author? Answer:
    Answer:	 Answer:	 Answer:	 Answer:

What do you and your partner have in common?

We both think that _____ .

We both think that _____ .

Ask your partner

Here are many questions. Choose about TEN that look interesting to you.

Ask and answer questions. When you answer, say "How about you?" or

"What do you think?"

How about you?

Ask your partner...	Ask your partner...	Ask your partner...	Ask your partner···
Where is your hometown? Answer:	What were you good at in high school? Answer:	Do you have a part time job? Answer:	What do you usually like doing after school? Answer:
What is one good memory you have of high school? Answer:	What is one of your good points of character? Answer:	What is one of your weak points of character? Answer:	What is one thing on your 'bucket list'? Answer:
What is something expensive you would like to buy? Answer:	Have you ever been to Hokkaido or Okinawa? Answer:	What kind of TV programs do you really dislike? Answer:	Have you ever broken a bone? Answer:
Do you have any irritating habits? Answer:	When was the last time you went to the movies? Answer:	Why do you want to study English? Answer:	What club or circle activities are you doing now? Answer:
How long does it take to commute to school? Answer:	Which foreign country would you like to go to? Answer:	What is your happiest memory of childhood? Answer:	Would you like to try bungee jumping in New Zealand? Answer:
Ask your partner... Answer:	Ask your partner... Answer:	Ask your partner... Answer:	Ask your partner... Answer:

What do you and your partner have in common?

We both think that _____ .

We both think that _____ .

Maybe you don't know anyone else in the class, so let's go round and ask each other some questions. Ask 5 questions.

Ask three other students. Do **NOT** ask the person sitting next to you!

First, you need to ask for your conversation partner's family name. Write it on the line.

Choose your questions carefully! Question 2 needs two answers!

Sorry, I didn't catch *that*...

How do you spell that?

What does ___ mean?

Could you tell me your family name?

Could you repeat that, please?

Questions:

Could you tell me...	My answers:	Mr /Miss: ___	Mr /Miss: ___	Mr /Miss: ___
1)... where is your hometown?	___ in ___ Prefecture.			
2)	1) 2)	1) 2)	1) 2)	1) 2)
3)				
4)				
5)				
6)				

What do you have in common?

Mr/Miss _____ and I both _____ .
Mr/Miss _____ and I both _____ .
Mr/Miss _____ and I both _____ .
Mr/Miss _____ and I both _____ .

Introducing myself

Write and tell me some interesting things about <u>YOU</u>. Write about:

1) Your hometown (where is it; why you like it).
2) Your hobbies or interests.
3) What you like doing in your free time.
4) What you are good at.
5) Your future dream.
6) A place you would like to visit (and why).

1. My hometown is

2. My hobbies or interests are

3. In my free time I like to

4. I think I am good at

5. My future dream is to

6. A place I would like to visit one day is

UNIT 2

Childhood memories

Bill and Yuko are talking about some memories of when they were kids.

First, find answers to these questions:

1) *Who was a tomboy in elementary school?*
2) *Who used to collect beetles?*
3) *Who had a great time in a foreign country?*
4) *Who wasn't allowed to keep a dog?*

Now, read the conversation with a partner:

1 Yuko: So what were you like as a kid?

  Bill: I was pretty small for my age, so I used to get bullied. Not too seriously, though. Bullying is a much bigger problem in Japan.

2 Yuko: Sounds tough. I used to really enjoy school, especially elementary school. I have many good memories. I was a bit of a tomboy. I often used to play with the neighborhood boys. Especially in the summer holidays.

  Bill: Oh, yeah? What did you use to do?

3 Yuko: Well, in summer we used to collect *kabutomushi...*

  Bill: *Kabutomushi?* What's that?

4 Yuko: Well, how do I explain? Some kind of beetle, I guess. What did you use to do in summer?

  Bill: My best memory of summer is taking a school trip to France.

5 Yuko: France? Wow! I wish we could have done that. How old were you?

  Bill: The last year of elementary school. About 11. It was the first time I met people who didn't speak English. And I remember I thought the food was really strange...

6 Yuko: One happy memory is my pet dog Chico. I used to take her for walks every morning before breakfast.

  Bill: I wish I had kept a dog when I was a kid. My parents wouldn't allow it. They only let me have some goldfish.

7 Yuko: One thing I regret, though, is that I didn't study harder. Maybe I was too busy playing with those neighborhood boys.

How about you? Take it in turns asking questions:

1) Were you called a nickname in elementary school?
2) What games did you use to play?
3) Do you have any unpleasant childhood memories?
4) Did you take any trips with your family?
5) Did you use to have a pet?
6) Is there anything you disliked doing when you were a kid?
7) Looking back, do you have any regrets?
8) Do you have anything in common with Bill or Yuko?

Memories of younger days

1. When I was a kid, I used to hate ____.
a) meat
b) green peppers
c) raw fish
d) carrots
e) dairy products such as milk and cheese
f) any green vegetables
g) _____

2. When I was in elementary school, I hated
    _____.
a) being bullied at school
b) staying indoors on summer days
c) going to a *juku* (cram school)
d) having to play a musical instrument
e) having to keep a summer diary
f) going to the dentist
g) _____

3. When I was a kid, I really used to like ____.
a) taking a trip with my family
b) taking a trip with my school
c) the school sports day
d) playing with the neighborhood kids
e) watching _____ on TV
f) _____

4. In the long summer holidays, I used to ____.
a) have a great time playing with my friends
b) be lonely because I didn't have many friends
c) be really busy doing homework
d) be really busy doing club activities
e) _____

5. When I was a little kid, I used to play ____.
a) *kakurenbou* (hide and seek)
b) *kankeri* (can-kicking)
c) *onigokko* (tag)
d) *semitori* (catching bugs)
e) *keidoro* (cops and robbers)
f) *mamagoto* (house)
g) _____

6. I _____ I could be a kid again.
a) sometimes wish   e) always wish
b) never wish   f) _____
c) rarely wish
d) often wish

7. When I was a little kid, I used to ___.
a) be a bit of a tomboy
b) be a cry-baby
c) be popular with my classmates
d) be really good at _____
e) really enjoy _____
f) _____

8. When I was a little kid, I used to collect _____.
a) bugs
b) stamps
c) trading cards
d) comic books
e) plastic models
f) _____

9. The most important influence on me when I was
    a child was _____.
a) my mother
b) my father
c) my older brother (or sister)
d) my home room teacher
e) my best friend

10. One thing I regret is that _____ in junior high
    school.
a) I didn't study harder
b) I didn't learn a musical instrument
c) I didn't play sports well
d) _____

11. Looking back, I wish I had ___ when I was
    younger.
a) studied harder
b) learned a musical instrument
c) played sports better
d) gone to swimming school
e) participated in club activities
f) _____

12. Looking back, my childhood was
    _____ .
a) great fun
b) pretty tough
c) good and bad
d) not a happy time

13. This was because _____.

Listen to the teacher talk about his or her childhood memories. Maybe these memories are from a long time ago!

Memories of childhood

What do you and your teacher have in common?

Teacher's name: _____

1. Memories of school.	
2. Memories of family.	
3. Memories of childhood friends.	
4. Memories of summer holidays.	
5. Memories of _____	

My childhood memories:

1	
2	
3	
4	
5	

I remember that I used to …

It's a long time ago, but one memory I have is when…

I can remember a time when …

Do you and your teacher have anything in common?

We both remember when _____.

We both used to _____.

Childhood memories

When do you think "childhood" begins and ends? Everyone may have a different opinion, but it is often thought to be from around the age of 3 or 4 to about 12 or 13 (before junior high school).

Do you have any special childhood memories? Do you remember your first day at kindergarten?

Talk with your partner and find out about his or her childhood memories.

Look at the boxes below.

1. Choose a number and say: "I'm going to talk about number *six.* "

Then say: "I remember that I ___" OR "I remember when ___"
OR "I remember that I **used** to ___" OR "One memory I have is when ___"

Remember to ask your partner's opinion. Say: "How about you?"
OR "what about you?"

1. A sport I used to play	2. A family holiday	3. After school
4. My first trip abroad	5. Summer holidays	6. A happy memory
7. My brother (s) and/or sister (s)	8. A pet I used to keep	9. My collection
10. My favorite teacher in my childhood	11. My first day at school	12. Something I used to really like doing
13. A sad or unpleasant memory	14. My best class	15. _____

2. Try to remember what your partner said and give a short summary to the class.

Childhood memories

People have good and bad memories, and things they regret or are envious about their childhood. Here are some interesting facts about childhood memories. Read the information and ask some questions.

The numbers are in percent.

Tough childhood experiences people had in summer	
1) So busy with club activities I had no free time	100
2) At a loose end every day	___
3) Getting sunburned	67.3
4) Too busy studying so didn't have free time	53.2
5) None of my friends invited me out to play	a

Which subject people regret not studying harder	
1) English	65.5
2) Arithmetic	___
3) Japanese	25.7
4) Social studies	26
5) Music	22.2

What adults are envious about concerning children today	
1) They can use the Internet	100
2) There is air-conditioning in classrooms	81.3
3) They can email their friends with cell phones	c
4) School meals are substantial	___
5) There are convenience stores close by	56.3

What people hated as a child, but love now	
1) Black coffee	e
2) Being quiet and alone	66.3
3) Studying	55.7
4) Cleaning their ears	___
5) The opposite sex	15.7

The problems in elementary and middle school people had	
1) Bullying	___
2) Large class size	31.1
3) The teacher quality	18.7
4) School violence	18.7
5) Corporal punishment	18.4
6) Truancy	17.6

The insects that most remind adults of childhood	
1) Fireflies	54.1
2) Dragonflies	___
3) Crickets	41.5
4) Cicadas	40.8
5) Rhinoceros beetles	37.9

Most disliked insects of people when they were children	
1) Cockroaches	62.4
2) Moths	10.3
3) Wasps or hornets	5.8
4) Flies	4.4
5) Stink-bugs	___

a) What percent of people were at a loose end every day in summer?
b) What percent of people regret not studying arithmetic harder in childhood?
c) What percent of people hated cleaning their ears when they were kids?
d) What percent of people felt bullying was a problem in childhood?
e) What percent of people are reminded by dragonflies of their childhood?
f) What percent of people disliked stink-bugs when they were kids?
g) What percent of people are envious that kids now have big school meals?
h) Now ask about a: _____
i) Now ask about c: _____
j) Now ask about e: _____
k) _____
l) _____

Childhood memories

People have good and bad memories, and things they regret or are envious about their childhood. Here are some interesting facts about childhood memories. Read the information and ask some questions.

The numbers are in percent.

Tough childhood experiences people had in summer	
1) So busy with club activities I had no free time	100
2) At a loose end every day	83.1
3) Getting sunburned	___
4) Too busy studying so didn't have free time	53.2
5) None of my friends invited me out to play	29.4

Which subject people regret not studying harder	
1) English	___
2) Arithmetic	37.1
3) Japanese	25.7
4) Social studies	b
5) Music	22.2

What adults are envious about concerning children today	
1) They can use the Internet	100
2) There is air-conditioning in classrooms	___
3) They can email their friends with cell phones	68.2
4) School meals are substantial	60.3
5) There are convenience stores close by	56.3

What people hated as a child, but love now	
1) Black coffee	100
2) Being quiet and alone	___
3) Studying	55.7
4) Cleaning my ears	17.6
5) The opposite sex	d

The problems in elementary and middle school people had	
1) Bullying	38.6
2) Large class size	31.1
3) The teacher quality	18.7
4) School violence	18.7
5) Corporal punishment	___
6) Truancy	17.6

The insects that most remind adults of childhood	
1) Fireflies	54.1
2) Dragonflies	47.8
3) Crickets	f
4) Cicadas	40.8
5) Rhinoceros beetles	___

Most disliked insects of people when they were children	
1) Cockroaches	___
2) Moths	10.3
3) Wasps or hornets	5.8
4) Flies	4.4
5) Stink-bugs	4

a) What percent of people disliked getting sunburned in summer?
b) What percent of people are envious that kids have air-conditioning in schools now?
c) What percent of people disliked being quiet and alone when they were kids?
d) What percent of people felt corporal punishment was a problem in childhood?
e) What percent of people regret not studying English harder in childhood?
f) What percent of people are reminded by rhinoceros beetles of their childhood?
g) What percent of people disliked cockroaches when they were kids?
h) Now ask about b: _____
i) Now ask about d: _____
j) Now ask about f: _____
k) _____
l) _____

I'm sure that you have many childhood memories both good and bad.

Ask and answer questions to learn a little about some childhood memories. What do you have in common?

Is it OK to ask you a few questions?

I **used** to really enjoy....

One thing I **used** to do....

Childlhood memories

Teacher's answers:	My answers:	Person 1	Person 2	person 3
1. What did you **use to** really enjoy doing when you were a kid? S/He **used to**				
2. What did you **use** to hate doing when you were a kid? S/He **used to**				
3. What did you **use** to be good at when you were in junior high school? S/He **used to**				
4. What do you **regret** about your childhood? 1) S/He **regrets** that s/he 2)	1) 2)			
5. What did you **use** to do on your birthday when you were a kid? 1) 2)	1) 2)			
6. _____ ?				

Mr/Miss _____ and I used to

Mr/Miss _____ and I used to

Mr/Miss _____ regret that we

20

Childhood memories

Go around the class and ask questions. You will need to think of the questions by looking at the sentence endings below. If someone answers "Yes", then write the full name on the line and then ask a follow-up question.

Find someone who···

1. _____ kept a dog when he/she was a kid.

2. _____ used to hate milk when he/she was in kindergarten.

3. _____ used to want to be a professional sportsperson when he/she was a kid.

4. _____ was bullied in junior high school.

5. _____ used to collect kabutomushi when he/she was a kid.

6. _____ used to hate going to the dentist.

7. _____ used to play a musical instrument when he/she was a kid.

8. _____ used to go camping with his/her family in summer.

9. _____

What were you like when you were a kid?

Work alone. Complete the sentences. Then compare with a partner. What do you have in common?

1. When I was a kid, I used to like _____.

2. When I was a kid, I often _____.

3. In elementary school I used to _____.

4. I used to hate _____.

5. I used to be _____ and _____.
    (use adjectives)

6. I _____ after school.

7. In summer I used to _____.

8. _____ used to make me cry.

9. I wish I could have _____.

10. If I could be 10 years old again, I_____.

Now ask your partner:

How about you?

22

Do you want to see a movie, sometime?

Look at the conversation between Bill and Yuko. Bill is inviting Yuko to go to the movies.

First, try to find the answers to these questions:

1) *Has Yuko been to the movies recently?*

2) *What kind of movies doesn't she like?*

3) *When is Bill busy? Why?*

4) *When and where will they meet?*

Now, read the conversation aloud with your partner.

1 Bill: Hi, Yuko. Are you busy these days?

 Yuko: Yeah, pretty busy. I sometimes have my new part time job and I do circle activities after school. Why do you ask?

2 Bill: I was wondering if you'd like to see a movie sometime this week.

 Yuko: I haven't seen a movie for ages. Sure. What's playing?

3 Bill: Well, I hear the new _____ movie is pretty good.

 Yuko: I don't think I know it. What kind of movie is it?

4 Bill: Well, it's an adventure movie. It's the latest blockbuster, so it should be fun.

 Yuko: I'm not so keen on blockbusters. And anyway, if it is so popular the theater will be very crowded.

5 Bill: OK. What kind of movies do you like?

 Yuko: Hmm. Comedies. Animation.

6 Bill: OK. How about the new _____ movie? It's a comedy and it starts playing this week.

 Yuko: Oh, I love _____! He's a great actor. Let's go!

7 Bill: How about Thursday?

 Yuko: Thursday? Let me think. . . Oh no, I'm sorry. I have to do my part time job. How about Friday?

8 Bill: Hmm. I was supposed to go bowling with my classmates. But I can change the day. OK. Let's go!

 Yuko: Great! Where shall we meet?

9 Bill: Well, if we go to the late show at 9pm, we can get cheaper tickets. Let's meet at McDonalds at 7 o'clock and have a burger before the movie starts.

 Yuko: OK. I'm looking forward to it.

10 Bill: Yeah, me too.

Now try and use these expressions in a sentence:

1. I was wondering if you'd like to _____.

2. I haven't _____ for ages.

3. I'm really looking forward to _____.

1. My favorite kinds of movies are _____.
a) action or adventure movies
b) comedies
c) love stories
d) animated movies
e) horror movies
f) American "Blockbusters"
g) suspense movies
h) foreign movies e.g French movies
i) _____

2. I have been to the movies ___ this year.
a) once
b) a few times
c) about 5 or 6 times
d) many times
e) so many times I can't count
f) not once
g) _____

3. The last time I went to a theater was _____.
a) last night
b) last week
c) a few weeks ago
d) last month
e) a few months ago
f) a few years ago
g) so long ago I can't remember
h) when I was a little kid with my family
i) _____

4. I would go to the movies more often if
_____.
a) I had some friends
b) I had more money
c) the movies were cheaper
d) there were movies I wanted to see
e) there were more foreign movies
f) the movie theater were closer to my home
g) I had more free time
h) _____

5. To be honest, watching movies is _____.
a) a waste of time
b) great fun
c) something I do from time to time
d) something I'm not keen on

6. If I could, I'd like to see _____ tonight.
a) an American movie
b) a Korean movie
c) a British movie
d) a French movie
e) a Japanese movie
f) a Chinese movie
g) _____

7. If I had the choice, I would _____ prefer to see
a dubbed movie rather than a subtitled movie.
a) definitely
b) probably
c) maybe
d) maybe not
e) probably not
f) definitely not

8. I think that 3D movies are_____.
a) a great idea
b) wonderful
c) a passing fashion
d) not good because they hurt my eyes
e) a waste of money
f) _____

9. I think I would _____ pay extra to see a 3D
movie rather than a 2D version.
a) definitely
b) probably
c) maybe
d) maybe not
e) probably not

_____

10. A movie playing now that I would like to see is:
_____

11. My favorite movie of all time is:
_____

12. My favorite movie star is:
_____

Blockbusters!

Here are some facts about the biggest movie hits from around the world.

Are you surprised by this Top Ten?

The biggest hits of all time!	
Movie	Year
1. Avatar	2009
2. _____	2019
3. Avatar: The Way of Water	2022
4. _____	1997
5. _____	2015
6. Avengers: Affinity War	2018
7. Spider Man: No Way Home	2021
8. Jurassic World	2015
9. _____	2019
10. Top Gun: Maverick	2022

Top 5 animated movies of all time	
Movie	Year
1. The Lion King	2019
2. Frozen 2	2019
3. _____	2023
4. Frozen	2013
5. Incredibles 2	2018

The biggest hit movies of the 1990s	
1. Titanic	1997
2. Jurassic Park	1993
3. _____	1999
4. The Lion King	1994
5. Independence Day	1996
6. _____	1990

The top 5 Japanese animated movies	
1. Demon Slayer	2020
2. Spirited Away	2001
3. Your Name	2016
4. _____	2022
5. Suzume	2022

First! Ask questions like this: What is the second most popular movie of all time?

1. How many of the "biggest hits of all time" movies have you seen?
2. Which one did you like the best?
3. Where did you see it? At home on TV, on a DVD, or at a theater?
4. Which did you like the least?
5. How about the "biggest hit movies of the 1990s"? How many of them have you seen?
6. Which one do you remember well?
7. Which do you prefer, action or animated movies?
8. How many of the foreign animated movies have you seen?
9. Which one did you like best?
10. How many of the Japanese animated movies have you seen?

Mr. Burden's favorite movies	
1. The Godfather	1972
2. The Shawshank Redemption	1994
3. The Godfather part 2	1974
4. Once Upon A Time In America	1984
5. Apocalypse Now	1979
6. Nomadland	2020
7. Three Billboards	2017

The number of movie theaters	
1. _____	_____
2. United States	40,246
3. _____	_____
4. Mexico	6,062
5. France	5,761
6. Germany	4,613
7. United Kingdom	4,046

1. Have you seen any of Mr. Burden's favorite movies?
2. Which country has the most/ third most movie theaters? How many?

Blockbusters!

Here are some facts about the biggest movie hits from around the world.

Are you surprised by this Top Ten?

The biggest hits of all time!	
Movie	Year
1. Avatar	2009
2. Avengers: Endgame	2019
3. _____	2022
4. Titanic	1997
5. Star Wars: Episode 7	2015
6. Avengers: Infinity Wars	2018
7. _____	2021
8. _____	2015
9. The Lion King	2019
10. _____	2023

Top 5 animated movies of all time	
Movie	Year
1. _____	2019
2. Frozen 2	2019
3. Super Mario Bros	2023
4. _____	2013
5. Incredibles 2	2018

The biggest hit movies of the 1990s	
1. _____	1997
2. _____	1993
3. Star Wars	1999
4. The Lion King	1994
5. Independence Day	1996
6. Ghost	1990

The top 5 Japanese animated movies	
1. Demon Slayer	2020
2. _____	2001
3. _____	2016
4. Slam Dunk	2022
5. Suzume	2022

First! Ask questions like this: What is the third most popular movie of all time?

1. How many of the "biggest hits of all time" movies have you seen
2. Which one did you like the best?
3. Where did you see it? At home on TV, on a DVD, or at a theater?
4. Which did you like the least?
5. How about the "biggest hit movies of the 1990s"? How many of them have you seen?
6. Which one do you remember well?
7. Which do you prefer, action or animated movies?
8. How many of the foreign animated movies have you seen?
9. Which one did you like best?
10. How many of the Japanese animated movies have you seen?

Mr. Burden's favorite movies	
1. The Godfather	1972
2. The Shawshank Redemption	1994
3. The Godfather part 2	1974
4. Once Upon A Time in America	1984
5. Apocalypse Now	1979
6. Nomadland	2020
7. Three Billboards	2017

The number of movie theaters	
1. China	54,164
2. _____	_____
3. India	11,000
4. _____	_____
5. France	5,761
6. Germany	4,613
7. United Kingdom	4,046

1. Have you seen any of Mr. Burden's favorite movies?
2. Which country has the second/fourth most movie theaters? How many?

Listen to the teacher talk about going to the movies. Do you have anything in common? Then ask two classmates:

Do you mind if I ask you some questions?

Going to the movies

	Teacher's answers:	My answers:	Classmate 1:	Classmate 2:
1) Do you like go to the movies?				
2) How often do you go to the theater?				
3) When was the last time?				
4) Which do you prefer, watching movies on DVD or going to a theater?				
5) What are three great movies you have seen on TV, DVD or video?	1) 2) 3)	1) 2) 3)	1) 2) 3)	1) 2) 3)
6) What's your favorite kind of movie?				
7) Is there anything playing now that you'd like to see?	1) 2)	1) 2)	1) 2)	1) 2)
8)				

Do you have anything in common?

Mr/ Miss and I _____

Mr/ Miss and I _____

Going to the movies!

People often invite their friends to go to the movies.
Here are some interesting facts about movie-going in Japan.
Read the information and ask some questions.

The numbers are in percent.

How often Japanese people go to the movies	
Once a year or less	22.5
Once every two or three months	___
Once every six months	19.3
Once a month	10.6
Two or three times a month	4.6
Have never been	___
Once a week or more	0.8

Who people went with	
By themselves	a
With spouse	___
With children, family	20
With friends	13.9
With boy/girlfriend	5.4

The main reasons people don't go more often	
No movies I wanted to see	25
Didn't have time to visit	24.6
Not interested in movies	c
No theaters close by	14.2
No-one to go with	6
Dislike movie theaters	2.9

How people found information about what is playing	
PC internet	88.3
Mobile phone website	18
At the theater	16.6
Newspaper	___
What's on magazine	3.9

The genres of movies people saw last year						
Age	First		Second		Third	
20s	Japanese animation (30.4)		Western SF, action (22.9)		J. Human drama	(20)
30s	Japanese animation (18.3)		Western SF, action (___)		J. Human drama	(7.1)
40s	Japanese human drama (18.3)		Western SF, action (15.8)		J. Animation	(13.3)
50s	Japanese human drama (20.7)		Western SF, action (19.5)		W. Human drama	(___)

The discount tickets people used	
Ladies' day	___
Discount coupon	39.1
First day of the month	31.3
Late show or midnight show	e

The kinds of theaters people use	
Cinema Multiplex (5 screens+)	74.9
Ordinary theaters (4 screens)	41.2
Independent theaters	10.7

a) What percent of people go the movies once every two or three months?

b) What percent of people have never been to a movie theater?

c) What percent of people go to the movies with their spouse?

d) What percent of people in their 30s watched Western Science Fiction or action movies?

e) What percent of people in their 50s watched Western human dramas?

f) What percent of people use Ladies' day discounts?

g) What percent of people get movie information from the newspaper?

h) Now ask about a: _____

i) Now ask about c: _____

j) Now ask about e: _____

k) _____

l) _____

Going to the movies!

People often invite their friends to go to the movies.
Here are some interesting facts about movie-going in Japan.
Read the information and ask some questions.

The numbers are in percent.

How often Japanese people go to the movies	
Once a year or less	___
Once every two or three months	19.8
Once every six months	19.3
Once a month	10.6
Two or three times a month	b
Have never been	2.3
Once a week or more	0.8

Who people went with	
By themselves	33.5
With spouse	26.3
With children, family	20
With friends	13.9
With boy/girlfriend	___

The main reasons people don't go more often	
No movies I wanted to see	25
Didn't have time to visit	24.6
Not interested in movies	19.3
No theaters close by	f
No-one to go with	___
Dislike movie theaters	2.9

How people found information about what is playing	
PC internet	88.3
Mobile phone website	18
At the theater	16.6
Newspaper	11.2
What's on magazine	3.9

The genres of movies people saw last year			
Age	First	Second	Third
20s	Japanese animation (___)	Western SF, action (22.9)	J. Human drama (20)
30s	Japanese animation (18.3)	Western SF, action (13.8)	J. Human drama (___)
40s	Japanese human drama (18.3)	Western SF, action (15.8)	J. Animation (13.3)
50s	Japanese human drama (20.7)	Western SF, action (d)	W. Human drama (13.7)

The discount tickets people used	
Ladies' day	46.3
Discount coupon	39.1
First day of the month	___
Late show or midnight show	30.3

The kinds of theaters people use	
Cinema Multiplex (5 screens+)	___
Ordinary theaters (4 screens)	41.2
Independent theaters	10.7

a) What percent of people go the movies once a year or less?
b) What percent of people go to the movies with their boyfriend or girlfriend?
c) What percent of people don't go to the movies because they have no-one to go with?
d) What percent of people in their 20s watched animated movies?
e) What percent of people in their 30s watched Japanese human dramas?
f) What percent of people use First day of the month discounts?
g) What percent of people go to a Cinema Multiplex?
h) Now ask about b: _____
i) Now ask about d: _____
j) Now ask about f: _____
k) _____
l) _____

Movie Review: The last movie I saw

Movie Title (in Japanese: Unmei no botan) English title: The Box

When and where did you see it: At home, last weekend on DVD.

The main actor or actress: Cameron Diaz

Overall grade out of 5:   ****   Length: About 2 hours

The story: ****   Genre: Suspense

The acting: ***

The action: ****

Your recommendation: An interesting movie with an exciting end. Rent this movie with a friend and imagine what you would do if someone offered you $1 million!

Your review:

This is a suspense movie set in the 1970s. Cameron Diaz, who is best known for appearing in comedies like *The Mask,* plays a middle-aged housewife who is partially disabled. She works as a teacher in a local high school but suddenly loses her job. Her husband works as a scientist for NASA but as a family they are not rich. One day, a strange man comes to the family home carrying a box. It is a mysterious box, with only a button on the top. The strange man says that if they push the button they will receive one million dollars. However, someone, somewhere will die. They will not know who or where. The family thinks very hard about whether to accept the strange man's proposition. Because they don't have much money, eventually they decide to take the money and they push the button. Then many terrible things start to happen. I won't tell you what happens next; you will have to see the movie.

This is an interesting movie that was originally a 30-minute TV program in the 1970s. The acting is quite good, but it is not a blockbuster as the movie was cheap to make. There are not many famous actors in it, so I was surprised the movie came to Japan. All the actors and actresses in the movie wore 1970s fashions, so some people had very bad hairstyles!

If you have the chance, I recommend renting this movie with a friend. It is a little scary in places, so maybe you will need to hold hands. This movie may be a little difficult to find but it is well worth the effort because it will certainly make you think!

If a strange man came to your house with a box and offered you a million dollars, what would you do? It's an interesting idea for a movie.

Movie Review: The last movie I saw

Movie Title:

When and where did you see it:

The main actor or actress:

Overall grade out of 5:   Length:

The story: Genre:

The acting:

The action:

Your recommendation:

Your review:

Go around the class and ask questions. You will need to think of the questions by looking at the sentence endings below. If someone answers "Yes", then write the full name on the line and then ask a follow-up question.

Find someone who···

1. _____ often sees movies at the theater.

2. _____ is a big fan of Johnny Depp.

3. _____ has seen all of the Harry Potter movies on TV, DVD or at the theater.

4. _____ has seen a 3D movie.

5. _____ has been to a "late show" movie recently.

6. _____ is a big fan of blockbusters.

7. _____ has a plan to go to the movies this weekend.

8. _____ prefers to see a DVD to going to the movie theater.

9. _____

UNIT 4

Vacation plans

Yuko is talking about her vacation plans. First, find the answers to these questions:

1) *Where is Yuko thinking of going?*
2) *Where does Bill recommend?*
3) *Why did he like it there?*
4) *What is one piece of advice Bill gives?*

Now, practice this conversation between Bill and Yuko.

1 Bill: Hi, Yuko. What's up?

  Yuko: Oh, nothing much. I'm really looking forward to the long vacation though.

2 Bill: Yeah, me too. Do you have any plans?

  Yuko: Yes, maybe I'll take a trip somewhere in Asia. How about you? Any plans yet?

3 Bill: No not really. I'll probably just do my part time job. I need the money.
           Where do you have in mind?

  Yuko: Well, I don't really know. I'm thinking about a trip to China.

4 Bill: You might like to go to Thailand. I went there last year. It was great.

  Yuko: Oh, yes? Why did you like it so much?

5 Bill: Well, for one thing, the food is delicious. The sightseeing in Bangkok is great, and
           the beaches in the south are fabulous, too.

  Yuko: Hmm. I'm not so keen on beaches...Do you have any advice?

6 Bill: Well, if you're traveling in Asia, you ought to check the weather. Sometimes
           there is a monsoon season.

  Yuko: "Monsoon"? What's that?

7 Bill: Er... Like the rainy season in Japan...

  Yuko: Oh, OK. You mean it rains a lot.

8 Bill: Yeah. And you should ask the doctor about injections or medicines.

  Yuko: Right. You really know a lot.

9 Bill: Perhaps you shouldn't go alone. It's not always safe at night. You ought to go
           with a friend.

  Yuko: Yeah, I agree. Um... I wonder who I should go with?

The conversation continues. Fill in the blanks:

Yuko: _____?

Bill: Apart from Thailand? I'd like to go to Cambodia or Laos sometime.

Yuko: _____?

Bill: Well, I hear the scenery is fantastic, and the people are really friendly.

About You...

1. Does traveling in Asia sound interesting to you?
2. Does Thailand sound good? Why or why not?
3. So, if you had the chance, where would you like to go on vacation?
4. Have you ever been abroad?

Traveling to foreign countries

1. I have been to a foreign country _____.
a) never, so far
b) only once, so far   e) many times
c) two or three times   f) _____
d) several times

2. If I have the chance, I want to visit _____.
a) somewhere in North America
b) somewhere in Europe
c) somewhere in Africa
d) somewhere in South America
e) somewhere in Asia
f) somewhere in Australia
g) nowhere

3. The **one** country I really want to go to if I have the chance is _____.

4. I would like to go there because:
_____
_____

5. If someone gave me a FREE airplane ticket to go abroad for more than two weeks, I would _____ go.
a) definitely
b) probably
c) maybe
d) probably not
e) definitely not

6. My parents would _____ worry if I went to a foreign country alone.
a) definitely
b) probably   d) probably not
c) maybe   e) _____

7. I would _____ like to go on a group tour with other Japanese people.
a) definitely
b) probably   e) _____
c) maybe
d) probably not

8. I would _____ like to live, work, or study in a foreign country for a year.
a) definitely   d) maybe not
b) probably   e) probably not
c) maybe   f) definitely not

9. To be honest, I _____.
a) really want to travel abroad
b) am not really interested in foreign travel
c) would rather travel in Japan

10. If I go to a foreign country, I will go because _____.
a) I want to go shopping
b) I want to meet interesting people
c) I want to try new, interesting food
d) I want to swim and relax on the beach
e) I want to go sightseeing
f) I want to speak English
g) _____

11. If I go abroad, I would be at a loss without _____.
a) some *cup ramens* in my bag
b) my Kindle, iPad, or similar device
c) my cell phone
d) my computer game console
e) Facebook or similar SNS
f) _____

12. If I go abroad, I will probably miss ____.
a) my parents or relatives
b) my friends
c) my car or bike
d) my own space
e) my computer
f) Japanese TV programs
g) Japanese food
h) _____

13. The biggest problem I will have if I go to a foreign country will be ____.
a) being understood in a foreign language
b) the unusual food
c) the different customs
d) the safety
e) the prices
f) knowing how to spend the evenings
g) finding my way around a new place
h) _____

14. I would like to go abroad _____.
a) one day in the distant future
b) in the next vacation
c) after I graduate
d) tomorrow
e) _____

15. I _____ agree that traveling abroad helps me understand my own country better.
a) definitely   d) perhaps don't
b) probably   e) _____
c) perhaps

Vacation Plans

What are you going to do in the next vacation? Do you have a travel plan?
Practice having a conversation like Bill and Yuko.

A: Hi, _____ . What's up?

B: Oh, nothing much. I'm really looking forward to the long vacation though.

A: Yeah, me too. Do you have any plans?

B: Yes, maybe I'll take a trip somewhere in _____①_____. How about you? Any plans yet?

A: No, not really. I'll probably just _____②_____. Where do you have in mind?

B: Well, I don't know yet. I hear _____③_____ is very popular.

A: You might like to go to _____④_____. I went there _____⑤_____. It was _____⑥_____!

B: Oh, really? What did you like the best?

A: Well, the _____⑦_____ was _____⑧_____, and the _____⑨_____ was _____⑩_____.

B: Sounds interesting. Do you have any advice?

A: Perhaps you _____⑪_____ _____⑫_____, and you really _____⑬_____ _____⑭_____.

B: Great. Thanks for the advice! Now I wonder who I should go with?

1. Asia
   Europe
   North America

2. do my part time job
   hang out with friends
   catch up on my studies

3. Vietnam
   Italy
   Canada

4. Bali
   Spain
   Mexico

5. last year
   with my family
   on a school trip

6. fantastic
   great
   wonderful

7. food
   beach
   scenery

8. really delicious
   very beautiful
   outstanding

9. sightseeing
   shopping
   nightlife

10. very interesting
    good and very cheap
    pretty exciting

11. ought to
    should
    really must

12. buy a guide book
    check the weather
    check on visas

13. shouldn't
    oughtn't to
    mustn't

14. go alone
    forget about travel insurance
    carry lots of cash in the evening

Tourist Destinations

Here are some interesting facts about world tourism. Let's read the facts and ask some questions.

The World's Top 10 Tourist destinations before COVID 19:

Country	Total visitors
1) France	84, 793, 217
2) United States	69, 832, 375
3) Spain	60, 717, 804
4) China	55, 797, 591
5) Italy	47, 759, 210
6) Turkey	37, 802, 642
7) Germany	31, 567, 893
8) United Kingdom	31, 206, 417
9) Russia	28, 671, 323
10) Thailand	26, 556, 801

Ask these questions:

1) Are you surprised by this Top 10?
2) Why do you think China had so many visitors?
3) What position do you think Japan is? Why?
4) Which of these countries would you most like to visit?
5) Which of these countries would you least like to visit?
6) _____?

Think of a famous DESTINATION in some of these countries. Ask your partner.

Country: Destination:

_____   _____
_____   _____
_____   _____
_____   _____
_____   _____

Most popular tourist cities in the world	
Place:	Number
1) Bangkok	22.78 million
2) Paris	19.10 million
3) London	19.09 million
4) Dubai	15.53 million
5) Singapore	14.67 million
6) Kuala Lumpur	13.79 million
7) New York	13.60 million
8) Istanbul	13.40 million

World's most popular theme parks

1) Magic Kingdom
2) Universal Islands of Adventure
3) Universal Studios
4) Disney's Hollywood Studios
5) Disneyland Park
6) Shanghai Disneyland

Most popular tourist destinations

1) The Colosseum, in Rome, Italy
2) The Louvre Museum, in Paris, France
3) The Vatican Museums, In Rome, Italy
4) The Statue of Liberty, in New York, USA
5) The Eifel Tower, in Paris, France
6) Sagrida Familia, in Barcelona, Spain
7) French Quarter, New Orleans, USA
8) Anne Frank House, Amsterdam, Netherlands
9) Grand Canal, Venice, Italy

The most World Heritage sites

1) Italy	58
2) China	56
3) Germany	52
4) Spain	49
5) France	49

1) Have you been to any of the theme parks?
2) Are there any you particularly want to visit?
3) Why do you think theme parks are so popular?
4) Do you know the names of any World Heritage sites in Italy? China? Germany? Spain?
5) Which site would you most like to visit?
6) How many sites are there in Japan, do you think?

Traveling Abroad

Most people like traveling abroad, or want to go to a foreign country.
Here are some interesting facts about traveling abroad for Japanese people.
Read the information and ask some questions.

The numbers are in percent.

Number of times people have been abroad	
1) Two or more times	25.4
2) Ten or more times	___
3) Five to nine times	19.9
4) Never	17.4
5) Once	15.5

Do people want to go abroad	
1) Want to go	49.4
2) Perhaps want to go	___
3) Perhaps don't want to	9.5
4) Don't want to go at all	3.9

What worries people before they go abroad	
1) They will get sick or robbed	a
2) They will have trouble being understood	95
3) What is the best way to carry money	79
4) Going abroad for the first time	78
5) The hotel facilities	74
6) Whether they can eat the food	70

Most popular weekend destination	
1) Seoul	59.3
2) Guam	___
3) Hawaii	34.8
4) Hong Kong	27.9
5) Taipei	25

What people want to do abroad	
1) Visiting tourist spots	84.7
2) Eating out	77.6
3) Visiting World Heritage sites	___
4) Shopping	53.6
5) Going to museums	c

Most popular longer destinations			
Male		Female	
1) Hawaii	53.7	1) Italy	e
2) Australia	52.8	2) Hawaii	59.2
3) Italy	52.4	3) Australia	55.9
4) France	43.4	4) France	55.3
5) USA	40.9	5) UK	___

Why people want to go abroad	
1) The yen exchange rate is good	57.2
2) There is a country they want to go to	46.3
3) There are cheap tours	23.9
4) Easy to get tickets on the Internet	19.7
5) A lot of LCC have started	___

Ideal vacation length	
1) 6 or 7 days	___
2) 8 to 14 days	29.7
3) 4 or 5 days	15.1
4) 15 days to a month	11.7
5) Longer than a month	5.3

a) What percent of people have been abroad ten or more times?
b) What percent of people perhaps want to go to a foreign destination?
c) What percent of people want to go to Guam on a long weekend?
d) What percent of people want to visit World Heritage sites on vacation?
e) What percent of women want to visit The UK?
f) What percent of people want to go abroad because of the increase in LCC?
g) What percent of people think the ideal length of a holiday is 6 or 7 days?
h) Now ask about a: _____
i) Now ask about c: _____
j) Now ask about e: _____
k) _____
l) _____

Traveling Abroad

Most people like traveling abroad, or want to go to a foreign country.
Here are some interesting facts about traveling abroad for Japanese people.
Read the information and ask some questions.

The numbers are in percent.

Number of times people have been abroad	
1) Two or more times	___
2) Ten or more times	21.5
3) Five to nine times	19.9
4) Never	b
5) Once	15.5

Do people want to go abroad	
1) Want to go	___
2) Perhaps want to go	37.2
3) Perhaps don't want to	9.5
4) Don't want to go at all	3.9

What worries people before they go abroad	
1) They will get sick or robbed	100
2) They will have trouble being understood	___
3) What is the best way to carry money	79
4) Going abroad for the first time	d
5) The hotel facilities	74
6) Whether they can eat the food	___

Most popular weekend destination	
1) Seoul	59.3
2) Guam	36.4
3) Hawaii	34.8
4) Hong Kong	27.9
5) Taipei	25

What people want to do abroad	
1) Visiting tourist spots	84.7
2) Eating out	77.6
3) Visiting World Heritage sites	72.2
4) Shopping	53.6
5) Going to museums	49.2

Most popular longer destinations				
Male		Female	
1) Hawaii	53.7	1) Italy	67.6
2) Australia	52.8	2) Hawaii	59.2
3) Italy	52.4	3) Australia	55.9
4) France	43.4	4) France	f
5) USA	___	5) UK	46.5

Why people want to go abroad	
1) The yen exchange rate is good	57.2
2) There is a country they want to go to	___
3) There are cheap tours	23.9
4) Easy to get tickets on the Internet	19.7
5) A lot of LCC have started	18.7

Ideal vacation length	
1) 6 or 7 days	37.3
2) 8 to 14 days	29.7
3) 4 or 5 days	15.1
4) 15 days to a month	___
5) Longer than a month	5.3

a) What percent of people have been abroad two or more times?

b) What percent of people want to go to a foreign destination?

c) What percent of people worry about being understood in a foreign country?

d) What percent of people worry whether they can eat the food in a foreign country?

e) What percent of men want to visit mainland USA?

f) What percent of people have a specific country in mind?

g) What percent of people think the ideal length of a holiday is 15 days to a month?

h) Now ask about b: _____

i) Now ask about d: _____

j) Now ask about f: _____

k) _____

l) _____

Giving advice: You should...

Here are some situations you might find yourself in when traveling abroad.

Give some advice. Use:

"You should..." or "You ought to..." or "You might like to..." or "You must..."
You can also use "You shouldn't..." or "You oughtn't to..." or "You mustn't..."

Student A is the student sitting on the left, and Student B is sitting on the right.

I've lost my way and can't find my hotel	I'm thinking of going to India	I'm thinking of going somewhere alone
I don't have much money but I need to buy a few souvenirs for family and friends	I want to find a cheap restaurant	I'm thinking of hiring a car while I'm abroad
I want to see an NBA game in America	I've left my bag on the train	I can't find my passport!
I'm lonely and would like to meet some Japanese people	I'm thinking of going somewhere in Asia but I am worried about the weather	I don't know whether to go to Australia or New Zealand

Can you think of two more situations? Write them here:

Giving advice: You should...

Here are some situations you might find yourself in when traveling abroad.

Give some advice. Use:

"You should..." or "You ought to..." or "You might like to..." or "You must..."
You can also use "You shouldn't..." or "You oughtn't to..." or "You mustn't..."

Student A is the student sitting on the left, and Student B is sitting on the right.

I've lost my cell phone!	I'm thinking of going some-where in South America	I want to take many pictures but my camera is old
I'm thinking of going hitch-hiking	I don't have much money and need a cheap place to stay	I want to see a Serie A soccer game in Italy
I'd really like to see a Broad-way musical in America	I can't find my wallet!	I really want to e-mail my friends back in Japan
I don't know if I should carry cash or take a credit card	I'm worried about going out in the evenings	I can't decide whether to go to America or Canada

Can you think of two more situations? Write them here:

Traveling abroad

Everybody wants to travel abroad sometime in the future. What do you have in common with your classmates?

Ask and answer some questions:

	My answers	Person 1	Person 2	Person 3
Teacher:				
1) Which country do you most want to visit?				
2) What do you want to do there?				
3) How long would you like to go?				
4) If you went abroad, what would you worry about?	1) 2)	1) 2)	1) 2)	1) 2)
5) What are two useful English phrases for traveling?	1) 2)	1) 2)	1) 2)	1) 2)
6) _____				
7) _____				

Sorry, could you say that again?

How do you spell that?

Do you have anything in common with your classmates?

Mr/Miss _____ and I _____

Mr/Miss _____ and I _____

Mr/Miss _____ and I _____

Go around the class and ask questions. You will need to think of the questions by looking at the sentence endings below. If someone answers "Yes", then write the full name on the line and then ask a follow-up question.

1. _____ has traveled somewhere in Asia.

2. _____ would like to do a homestay abroad.

3. _____ wants to work in the tourism industry.

4. _____ has been to two foreign countries.

5. _____ wants to go somewhere in Europe.

6. _____ wants to visit South America.

7. _____ would miss his/her parents if he/she went abroad.

8. _____ is interested in visiting Cambodia, Vietnam or Laos.

9. _____ has been somewhere exotic.

10. _____ knows what the capital of Australia is.

11. _____ would like to go bungee jumping in New Zealand.

12. _____

Where I would like to go in the future

Write and tell me about where you would like to travel in the world and why. Please write about:

1) Your experiences, if any, of traveling abroad up to now.
2) Where you would really like to go.
3) Your reasons for your choice.
4) A place you wouldn't want to go to.
5) When you would like to go abroad.

1. *Until now, I have*

2. *If I have the chance, I*

3. *I would like to go there because*

4. *I wouldn't like to go to*

5. *I would like to go abroad*

Snapshot 1: Traveling abroad

British people have enjoyed traveling abroad for nearly two hundred years. In the 1840s, rich young people, usually men, used to take part in the "Grand Tour" traveling in Europe for between two and four years. It was part of their education, and they visited famous cities including Paris, Florence, Rome and Vienna. They learned about the culture, art, language and manners.

Nowadays, a "Gap Year" is very popular for young students, both male and female. A gap year is an *empty year* between finishing high school and entering university, and for some universities it is almost compulsory to get "life experience." Many people do voluntary work abroad, or travel to exotic countries and learn a foreign language; something they might not have a chance to do again in their busy lives after university.

Thirty years ago, many students were happy to go "Euro-railing" in summer. This was traveling around Europe for a month by train with a special student pass. It was a good chance to make friends and see the sights of Europe. Euro-railing has recently become popular with older people as there are big discounts for people over 60 years old. These days, many young people prefer more exotic countries in Asia like Thailand, or go to India, or even go as far as Australia and get a "working holiday" visa for a month or so in summer.

Families also take foreign trips. Many people in Britain have long summer vacations, compared to Japanese workers, so many families like to go camping. Many families take their car on a ferry to France and stay at large, luxurious campsites. These are called "Fresh Air Hotels" in French and they often have swimming pools and restaurants.

The package tour originated in Britain becoming popular in the 1960s. You pay for your plane ticket, hotel, and even your food before you leave home. Everything is included in the price. Popular locations include beach resorts in Spain, Greece or Turkey, or taking a cruise along the River Nile in Egypt. The Low Cost Carrier (LCC) started in Britain too, and you can fly almost anywhere in Europe in a couple of hours or so. Now almost every city has an airport with cheap airplane tickets to Spain, Greece and Turkey.

Of course, British people are very lucky because they speak English. British people are often very lazy about learning foreign languages. School children in England are supposed to learn French, but even after seven years many can only remember "bonjour". British people are also suspicious of foreign food and often will not eat local food in southern Europe such as squid or octopus. So, you can find restaurants in Spain and Greece that sell terrible *English* food with 'french fries' (fried potatoes) with everything. These restaurants will be full, but everyone will be British!

Take turns with your partner to explain these key words:

Grand Tour Gap year exotic Fresh Air Hotels Package Tours LCC

UNIT 5

What are you doing on Saturday night?

Bill is asking Yuko about her weekend plans. First, find the answers to these questions:

1) *Does Yuko accept or decline Bill's first invitation?*

2) *What reason does she give?*

3) *What is Yuko not keen on?*

4) *What does she suggest?*

Now, practice the conversation.

1 Bill: Hi, Yuko. I haven't seen you for a while.

  Yuko: Oh, hello, Bill. Long time no see.

2 Bill: How are you? Busy these days?

  Yuko: I'm fine, thanks. No, I'm not so busy.

3 Bill: Do you have any plans for the weekend?

  Yuko: No, not really.

4 Bill: Would you like to go bowling on Friday night?

  Yuko: Oh. You know what? I always have my part time job on Friday evenings. I'm not busy on Saturday evening, though.

5 Bill: I hear there's a punk rock band from England playing at *Happy Bananas* in Kurashiki...

  Yuko: Punk rock band? I'm not too keen on punk.

6 Bill: (Disappointed face) Oh, never mind.

  Yuko: Wait a minute. Let's check online. How about this?

7 Bill: What?

  Yuko: There's a jazz concert at the *Blue Note Club* in Okayama.

8 Bill: Jazz?

  Yuko: Yes. I really like jazz. I thought I told you that.

9 Bill: Great! Let's go. Where shall we meet?

  Yuko: Well, the *Blue Note Club* is not far from the station. Let's meet in front of Okayama station at the fountain at about 6.30.

10 Bill: OK. I'm looking forward to it.

  Yuko: Me too. See you then. Don't be late.

Ask your partner:

1) Have you invited a friend to do anything recently?

2) Did your friend accept or decline?

3) What is a fun activity to do with your friends?

4) Where is a good meeting place in your town?

Free time activities

1. My free time is usually _____.
a) every day after school
b) only at weekends
c) one or two evenings a week
d) two or three evenings a week
e) _____

2. This weekend, I would really like to ____.
a) see a movie
b) go to *karaoke* with my friends
c) relax in front of the TV
d) go to a livehouse or concert
e) eat out with my friends
f) play or see some sports
g) _____

3. After school, I usually _____.
a) just go straight home
b) do club or circle activities
c) go to my part time job
d) hang out with friends on campus
e) hang out at the shops
f) browse the Internet at school
g) _____

4. For me, going window shopping or browsing in book stores is _____.
a) a great way to spend time
b) a waste of time
c) OK for a short while
d) something I like to do occasionally
e) really boring
f) great fun

5. For me, spending free time with my family would be _____.
a) a great way to spend time
b) OK for a short while
c) something I like to do occasionally
d) really boring
e) great fun
f) _____

6. I'm not keen on spending my free time _____.
a) watching movies
b) surfing the Internet
c) chatting with classmates
d) sitting in front of the TV
e) reading books, magazines or comics
f) _____

7. If it is raining on my free day, I _____.
a) just stay home and watch TV
b) go to the gym or indoor swimming pool
c) carry on as usual
d) just sleep
e) get very bored
f) clean my room, or do housework
g) just chat online or surf the 'net

8. A great weekend would be _____.
a) going to a hot spring with my family
b) going with my friends to Universal Studios in Osaka
c) taking a trip somewhere
d) just spending time alone
e) just hanging out with friends
f) _____

9. I would really dislike to _____ on weekends.
a) study English
b) do a part time job
c) go to *karaoke*
d) go _____
e) clean or do housework
f) _____

10. Tonight, I think I will:
_____

11. This weekend I'm looking forward to:
_____

12. This weekend I'm not looking forward to:
_____

Accepting and decling. Politely!

What are you doing this Saturday night? Any plans?

Today it is Thursday. Ask your partner about their weekend plans.

A: Hi, _____.

B: Oh, hello, _____.

A: How are you? Busy these days?

B: I'm fine, thanks. No, I'm not so busy. Just studying hard at university...

A: Do you have any plans for the weekend?

B: No, not really. Do you have something in mind?

A: *Would you like to* _____ on Friday night?

B: Friday night? I'm sorry, but I'm going to _____.

A: That's too bad. How about Saturday? *Why don't we* go to a concert on Saturday night?

B: Sounds good!

A: There's a/an _____ concert at _____.

B: _____? I'm not too keen on _____...

A: (Disappointed face) OK. How about this? There's a concert at _____.

B: What's playing?

A: _____.

B: Sounds good! How much is the ticket?

A: It's _____ yen.

B: Er... That's pretty expensive.

A: OK. Let me pay!

B: Great! Thanks. What time shall we meet?

A: The concert starts at _____. Let's meet at _____ at _____.

B: OK. I'm looking forward to it.

A: Me too.

Now make your own conversation. Remember! If you decline, you
ought to give a reason. It's more polite that way.

Start like this:

A: Hi, _____. How are you doing these days?

Live Jazz
At Blue Note Club
Okayama

Saturday March 31st at 8.30p.m

2000 yen including one drink!

Live

African

Drumming!!

Kurashiki Citizens' Hall

Saturday March 31st
3pm
Tickets: 2,500 yen

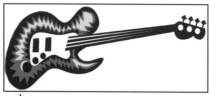

Blue Aeroplanes

Live from UK
Great British punk rock

Live at:

Happy Bananas 9:00 PM

Saturday March 31st

2,500 yen advance/3,000 yen on the door
Kurashiki

Rock 'N' Roll

Great 1950's Dance Music

Live at Pete's Palace
Okayama
Saturday March 31
Start time: 10 pm
1,000 yen inc. one drink

Making invitations: Would you like to ... sometime this week?

When we are invited, we can either accept or decline.

If we decline, we nearly always give a reason.

Look at the two short conversations and practice:

What do these mean?

accept _____

decline _____

A: Would you like to *see a movie* sometime this week?
B: Sure, sounds great. I haven't seen a movie for ages. What day?
A: How about *Thursday evening* ?
B: *Thursday evening* ? OK. Let's do it. What time?
A: Let's meet *at the fountain by Okayama station* at 7.
B: OK, I'm looking forward to it.
A: Yeah, me too.

A: Would you like to *see a movie* sometime this week?
B: Sure, sounds great. I haven't seen a movie for ages. What day?
A: How about *Thursday evening* ?
B: *Thursday evening* ? I'm sorry, but I *have to do my part time job* then.
A: Oh, that's too bad. *Maybe another time, then* .
B: OK, I'm looking forward to it.
A: Yeah, me too.

Now invite four classmates to do something sometime this week. REMEMBER! Do not invite the person sitting next to you.

	Person 1 Name _____	Person 2 Name _____	Person 3 Name _____	Person 4 Name _____
1. Would you like to _____ _____ ?	Accept/decline: _____ Decline: reason _____ Accept: doing? _____ Accept: time/place _____			
2. Why don't we _____ ?		Accept/decline: _____ Decline: reason _____ Accept: doing? _____ Accept: time/place _____		
3. Do you want to _____ ?			Accept/decline: _____ Decline: reason _____ Accept: doing? _____ Accept: time/place _____	
4. How about if we _____ ?				Accept/decline: _____ Decline: reason _____ Accept: doing? _____ Accept: time/place _____

Snapshot 2: Free time activities in Britain

What do people like to do in their free time? In Britain, working people usually do less than a 40-hour week these days, so they have plenty of time to do their favorite pastimes.

On weekends, many young people over eighteen and students spend Saturday night in the pub or bars. Unfortunately, many young people, both men and women, drink a lot of alcohol at the weekend which can make some cities look a little unsafe on Saturday nights. However, recently, the number of young people who do not drink alcohol is increasing.

While young Japanese may not drink as much as people in Britain, Japanese young people often say they spend Sunday "sleeping". Do you? Do they really mean sleeping? I think perhaps they mean "taking it easy" by watching TV, listening to music, taking naps, talking with friends on their cell phones, or surfing the Internet.

Going to the movies is very popular in Britain. Most towns have one or two "Multiplex" movie theaters with up to 14 screens. Hollywood blockbusters are most popular, as in many countries all over the world, but "art-house" theaters are popular too which show foreign movies which are dubbed or have English subtitles. As in many counties, going to the movies is a popular way of having a date.

Shopping used to be the most common way of spending Saturdays, but recently many people shop online so walking around city centers is not so popular these days. Many people would rather watch or play sports. Going to see a football (soccer) game is very popular, although getting tickets to see a Premier League football game can be very expensive. There are 92 professional football teams just in England and Wales (15 or so more in Scotland), so most major cities have at least one team. London has at least 14 teams. Other popular sports are rugby in winter and cricket in summer, but cricket is not popular in Japan. It is similar to baseball, and it has recently become very popular with young people as it can be very exciting. Although Britain took part in the 2023 World Baseball Classic, they lost by 10 runs to Canada!

Bowling is not so popular in England and karaoke has not really taken off because many people are terrible at singing: why pay money to hear someone who can't sing? People do like to eat out and themed restaurant chains are quite fashionable at the moment. Unfortunately, eating out is pretty expensive in Britain for families, so it is often only on special occasions like birthdays. Going to a pizza restaurant is popular for kids' birthday parties.

English language textbooks used to ask "What are your hobbies?" But these days, many people don't really have hobbies. In the old days, kids used to like collecting things like stamps, but these days most kids and young adults prefer games, the Internet, streaming, TV, or music to traditional "educational" hobbies like collecting something or playing a musical instrument. So, instead of asking, "What are your hobbies?" perhaps we should say, "What do you like to do in your free time?" How about you? Do you have a "hobby"? Do you have anything in common with young people in Britain?

1) What do the underlined words mean? Can you find another English word?
2) How is Britain different from Japan?

In my free time

Write and tell me about how you like to spend your free time and why. Please write about:

1) What you usually do at the weekend.
2) If you have the chance, what would you like to do this weekend.
3) What you are not keen on doing at the weekend.
4) What you think you will probably do this weekend.
5) What would be a great weekend.

1. On the weekend, I usually

2. If I have the chance, this weekend I would like to

3. I'm not keen on spending my free time

4. This weekend, I think I'll probably

5. For me, a great weekend would be

Aim to write at least 15 lines.

UNIT 6

What annoys you?

First, read the conversation quickly, and find the answers to these questions:

1) *How does Yuko look?*
2) *What is Yuko's problem?*
3) *What does Yuko hate?*
4) *What bothers Bill?*

Now practice the conversation between Bill and Yuko:

1 Bill: Hey Yuko. What's up? You look kind of annoyed.

Yuko: Oh, hi Bill. Yeah, I guess I am pretty upset. I'm waiting for my friend and she hasn't turned up yet.

2 Bill: Has she forgotten the day?

Yuko: No, she's only 5 minutes late so far. She's often late. It really irritates me...

3 Bill: Just 5 minutes? Relax. Take it easy. Maybe she's held up in traffic... It's hard to arrive exactly on time.

Yuko: Yeah, I know that, but it really irritates me when people don't come on time.

4 Bill: Wow, are you always so punctual?

Yuko: Yeah, I'm always on time. Like a clock. I think it is important to be reliable.

5 Bill: Well, I guess I'm more easygoing than you.

Yuko: Yeah, I guess it is my weakpoint. Do you have any?

6 Bill: I don't know... Maybe I'm a little tight-fisted, and a bit lazy, I guess.

Yuko: Tight-fisted?

7 Bill: You know, people who are not keen on spending money.

Yuko: Oh, OK. In Japanese we say "*ketchi*". So, what bothers you in Japan?

8 Bill: In Japan, I really dislike people who drop trash. I cycle a lot, and I sometimes see fast-food and soft drink containers thrown out of car windows. That bothers me. Also, it annoys me when people stand still on the escalator when I'm in a hurry. In England we usually don't just stand...

Yuko: Really? That doesn't bother me at all!

9 Bill: Generally though, I think that Japan is a pretty easy country to live in.

How about you? Ask your partner these questions:

1) What is something that annoys or irritates you?
2) Do people not arriving on time irritate you?
3) Are you tight-fisted?
4) Do you know anyone else who is?
5) Do you share any of Bill's feelings?
6) What do you usually do on escalators?

What kind of a person are you?

1. I think I am _____.
a) pretty easygoing
b) a person who easily gets irritated
c) someone who never gets annoyed
d) a person who is always annoyed
e) _____

2. I think I am _____.
a) very friendly
b) sometimes sociable
c) good at telling jokes
d) poor at telling jokes
e) not very friendly or sociable
f) sometimes moody or irritable
g) _____

3. I think a strong point of my character is that I
   am _____.
a) friendly and outgoing
b) kind and considerate
c) generous
d) easygoing
e) dependable
f) _____

4. Maybe a weak point of my character is that I
   am _____.
a) short tempered
b) boring
c) not very punctual
d) unsociable
e) forgetful
f) tight-fisted
g) unreliable
h) _____

5. If I saw someone do something that annoys or
   irritates me, I would _____.
a) politely ask the person to stop
b) tell the person to stop
c) get angry and start shouting
d) do nothing
e) pretend not to notice
f) _____

6. On an escalator I usually _____
a) walk quickly up or down
b) just stand and wait
c) stand on the left
d) stand on the right
e) ask the person in front to move
f) just wait patiently
g) get irritated
h) _____

7. I get irritated _____.
a) when people chat at the movies
b) when people talk loudly on their cell phone
c) when people smoke around me
d) when _____

8. I am a person who _____.
a) never irritates others
b) often irritates others
c) occasionally irritates others
d) usually irritates others
e) rarely irritates others

9. I _____ get irritated with my family easily.
a) often
b) never
c) usually   e) occasionally
d) always   f) _____

10. Two irritating habits I have are that I:
a) _____
b) _____

11. One thing that annoys me about other stu-
    dents is when they _____.
a) sleep in class   g) _____
b) don't do homework and ask to see mine
c) play with their phones under the desk
d) make a lot of noise in the library
e) chat with their friends at the back
f) don't buy the textbook

12. One thing that irritates me about teachers is
    when they _____.
a) come to class early
b) come to class late
c) only talk the whole time
d) use the microphone
e) write unclearly on the blackboard
f) _____

You look kind of annoyed

A: Hey _____. What's up? You look **kind of** annoyed.

B: Oh, hi _____. Yeah, **I guess** I am **pretty** upset. I'm waiting ____①____ and ____②____ hasn't turned up yet.

A: Have you been waiting long?

B: No, ____③____ late so far.

A: Just ____ minutes? Relax take it easy. In England it is unusual for anything to arrive exactly on time. Especially public transport, like trains.

B: Yeah I know that, but this is Japan, and ____④____. I ____⑤____.

A: **For me, I really dislike it when** ____⑥____.

B: Me too. **I also dislike it when** students ____⑦____.

A: That ____⑧____.

B: Is there anything you do that bothers other people?

A: Well, I often forget to ____⑨____, that really bothers my ____⑩____. How would you describe your character?

B: I enjoy ____⑪____, so I guess I'm ____⑫____. How about you?

A: The opposite! I find it difficult to ____⑬____, so mabe I'm kind of ____⑭____.

---

1. for the bus
   for a train
   for my boyfriend/girlfriend
   YOU

2. it
   he
   she
   YOU

3. it's only 3 minutes
   it's just 5 minutes
   he/she's only 10 minutes
   YOU

4. I'm not happy
   I'm annoyed
   I'm angry
   YOU

5. get annoyed when buses are late
   really dislike it when trains are not on time
   get really irritated when people are unpunctual
   YOU

6. people put their bags on seats
   people don't use lights on bicycles
   people throw trash out of car windows
   YOU

7. secretly play games
   sleep in class
   ask to see my homework
   YOU

8. doesn't bother me
   makes me a bit annoyed
   is not so bad
   YOU

9. turn off lights at home
   hang up my clothes
   wash the dishes
   YOU

10. mother
    roommates
    parents
    YOU

11. studying English
    watching Netflix
    going to karaoke
    YOU

12. pretty serious
    relaxing a lot
    quite sociable
    YOU

13. study at the weekend
    stay at home on weekends
    meet other people
    YOU

14. lazy
    active
    unsociable recently
    YOU

What irritates you?

Everybody gets irritated with bad habits, bad manners, and thoughtless behavior. Here are some interesting facts about what irritates Japanese people. Read the information and ask some questions.

The numbers are in percent.

Actions of family members that are irritating	
1) Being in a bad mood for no reason	100
2) Nagging	___
3) Loud snoring	50.6
4) Scattering things around the room	44.3
5) Frequently switching the TV channel	32.4
6) Forgetting to turn off the toilet light	a

Annoying chopstick habits	
1) *Hotokebashi* - standing chopsticks up in a rice bowl	100
2) *Sashibashi* - pointing at people or things with chopsticks	___
3) *Tatakibashi* - making a noise by striking dishes with chopsticks	90.1
4) *Neburibashi* - licking your chopsticks	71.5
5) *Awasebashi* - passing food from chopsticks to chopsticks	c
6) *Mayoibashi* - Hovering chopsticks over food	56.1

Bad manners that irritate people on the train	
1) Young or fit people sitting in the priority seats	___
2) Not squeezing up on the bench seats when the train is crowded	82.8
3) Not moving away from the doors	79.7
4) Not following telephone manners	78.8
5) Leaky headphones	___
6) Putting on make up in the train	e

Bad manners of kids	
1) Standing on train seats with their shoes on	89.6
2) Pushing into lines on the train	___
3) Littering	76.5
4) Putting plates back on the conveyor belt in sushi restaurants	74.7
5) Making a racket in public	69.8

a) What percent of people find nagging by family members irritating?
b) What percent of people get annoyed when others point at someone or something with their chopsticks?
c) What percent of people get annoyed when young or fit people sit in the priority seats?
d) What percent of people get irritated by kids who push into lines?
e) What percent of people get irritated by leaky headphones on the train?
f) What percent of people: _____
g) Now ask about a: _____
h) Now ask about c: _____
i) Now ask about e: _____
j) _____
k) _____

What irritates you?

Everybody gets irritated with bad habits, bad manners, and thoughtless behavior. Here are some interesting facts about what irritates Japanese people. Read the information and ask some questions.

The numbers are in percent.

Actions of family members that are irritating	
1) Being in a bad mood for no reason	100
2) Nagging	76.2
3) Loud snoring	___
4) Scattering things around the room	b
5) Frequently switching the TV channel	___
6) Forgetting to turn off the toilet light	25.8

Annoying chopstick habits	
1) *Hotokebashi* - standing chopsticks up in a rice bowl	100
2) *Sashibashi* - pointing at people or things with chopsticks	91.1
3) *Tatakibashi* - making a noise by striking dishes with chopsticks	90.1
4) *Neburibashi* - licking your chopsticks	___
5) *Awasebashi* - passing food from chopsticks to chopsticks	68.3
6) *Mayoibashi* - Hovering chopsticks over food	d

Bad manners that irritate people on the train	
1) Young or fit people sitting in the priority seats	83.7
2) Not squeezing up on the bench seats when the train is crowded	82.8
3) Not moving away from the doors	___
4) Not following telephone manners	78.8
5) Leaky headphones	67.2
6) Putting on make up in the train	66.8

Bad manners of kids	
1) Standing on train seats with their shoes on	f
2) Pushing into lines on the train	78.4
3) Littering	___
4) Putting plates back on the conveyor belt in sushi restaurants	74.7
5) Making a racket in public	69.8

a) What percent of people get annoyed by loud snoring?

b) What percent of people get irritated at people who lick their chopsticks?

c) What percent of people get annoyed when people don't move away from the train doors?

d) What percent of people get annoyed by kids who litter?

e) What percent of people get annoyed when family members frequently change the TV channel?

f) What percent of people: _____

g) Now ask about b: _____

h) Now ask about d: _____

i) Now ask about f: _____

j) _____

k) _____

Do you ever...?

What sort of person are you?

Put a circle (O) in the correct box for your answer.

Then, ask your partner. Put a triangle (▽) in the correct box for his or her answer.

If you have a 0 and a ▽ in the same box, you have something in common.

Do you ever feel ...?	1	2	3	4	5	6
1. angry when someone uses their cell phone on the train						
2. annoyed when people drop trash on the street						
3. irritated when you have to wait a long time at a red traffic light						
4. bothered when cyclists ride their bicycles side by side						
5. irritated when other students are sleeping in class						
6. bothered when people don't wait in line at the train station						
7. annoyed at slow Internet service, or when you cannot use wifi						
8. angry when car drivers park in the "disabled" parking space						
9. bothered when you have to wait at a supermarket checkout						
10. irriated when people check their phones in the movie theater						
11. bothered when the teacher is late for class						
12. irritated when the neighbors play loud music or talk in loud voices						
13. bothered when dog-owners don't clean up after their dog						
14. angry when car drivers keep their engines running when parked						
15. annoyed at noisy earphones on the train or bus						
16. . .						
17. . .						

1= No, never. This doesn't bother me at all	What about you?
2= No, hardly ever. This doesn't bother me	What do you think?
3= Not usually. It doesn't bother me much	How about you?
4= Yes, sometimes. But it depends	
5= Yes, usually. It kind of annoys me	
6= Yes, always. That really annoys me!	

Add up your scores. Do you get bothered easily?

How many scores of 6 did you get? _____

How many scores of 5 did you get? _____

What did you find in common? For example:

It really annoys us when *someone uses their cell phone on the train.*

1) It really annnoys us when _____.

2) It kind of annoys us when _____.

3) It sometimes bothers us when _____.

4) It doesn't bother us much when _____.

5) It hardly ever bothers us when _____.

6) It doesn't bother us at all when _____.

Listen to the teacher talk about pet hates. Do you have anything in common with the teacher?

Example: I really hate it when car drivers turn left without indicating.

My pet hates

1

2

3

4

5

Teacher's name: _____

One thing that really annoys me is when …

It really irritates me when (people) …

I really dislike it when people …

It kind of bothers me when my father/mother/ friend/classmate …

Pet hate number 1
It really annoys me when …

Pet hate number 2
It really irritates me when …

Pet hate number 3
I really dislike it when …

Pet hate number 4
It kind of bothers me when …

Pet hate number 5
I get a little annoyed when …

Do you and your teacher have anything in common?

We both get really annoyed when _____.

We both _____.

When are you...?

Look at the words below: Are there any words you don't know? Perhaps your partner knows.
Ask him or her:

"Can you explain what **CONFIDENT** *means in English?"*
Answer like this:
"Well, you feel **CONFIDENT** *when you are* **GOOD AT SOMETHING"**

happy	bored	lonely	relaxed	sad	interested	shy
angry	comfortable	nervous	depressed	uncomfortable		nostalgic

Fill in the table below using the words in the box.

other words:

1) I'm _____	when I listen to hip hop music
2) I'm _____	when I read a newspaper or novel
3) I'm _____	when I talk to members of the opposite sex
4) I'm _____	when I come to this class
5) I'm _____	when I watch TV alone at home
6) I'm _____	when I spend time with my family
7) I'm _____	when I have to do a test
8) I'm _____	when I see a romantic movie
9) I'm _____	when I meet new people
10) I'm _____	when I meet junior high school friends
11) I'm _____	when I do a part time job
12) I'm _____	when my friends are late
13) I'm _____	when I get up on Monday mornings
14) I'm _____	when I talk in English with a classmate
15) I'm _____	when I _____

other words:
embarrassed
worried
afraid
lethargic
disappointed
enthusiastic
glad
irritable

Now cover your answers and ask your partner questions like this:

A: When are you *lonely* ?
B: I *sometimes* feel *lonely* when *I watch TV alone*. How about you?
A: Me too

Oh, I don't. I feel *lonely* when I _____

What do you and your partner have in common? Tell the class:

We both feel _____ when we _____.

"Pet hates"

This is a list of pet hates from www.getannoyed.com. These pet hates come from America. Do you have anything in common with American pet hates? Maybe some of them you have never experienced.

Which of these pet hates:
a) really annoys/irritates/bothers you
b) annoys/bothers or irritates you a little
c) doesn't bother/irritate/annoy you
d) have never experienced

1) Drivers who don't use a turn signal.

2) People who sit next to you on public transportation even when there are other seats available.

3) Family members who drink milk or juice straight from the carton.

4) People who are noisy eaters.

5) People who don't cover their mouth while sneezing or coughing.

6) Family members who leave the cap off the toothpaste.

7) People who read over your shoulder on public transportation.

8) People who don't know the difference between "your/you're" and "they're/their".

9) People who pop and smack their chewing gum.

10) People who put their feet out of the car window.

11) People who don't wash their hands after using the restroom.

12) People who turn their stereos up full blast in their apartment building and have no consideration of others.

13) People who whistle or sing to themselves.

14) People who won't take their child out of a restaurant when they are crying, screaming, and so on.

15) People who think the seat next to them is a place to put down their bag on a crowded bus.

Learning English

Bill and Yuko are talking about world languages and studying English.

First, find the answers to these questions:

1) *Why are many languages dying out?*

2) *Which language has the most speakers?*

3) *How many different languages are there in the world?*

4) *What might happen in 100 years?*

Now read the conversation with your partner:

1 Yuko: I've been reading this interesting book.

  Bill: Oh, yes? What is it about?

2 Yuko: It's about how many languages in the world are dying out.

  Bill: Dying out? Why's that?

3 Yuko: Well, one reason is that too many people are being forced to speak English.

  Bill: Forced? But they can still speak their first language at home can't they? And is it only English that is the problem?

4 Yuko: No not only English, but to get jobs, they have to move to bigger cities where English is the language of business. So they don't get much chance to speak the local language. They get married and their kids are brought up to speak English not their mother tongue. So in some places, languages are disappearing.

  Bill: Mmm. That's terrible. I didn't know that speaking English caused so many problems.

5 Yuko: Yes, I like learning English, and think it will help me get a job, and is useful for traveling. But on the other hand, if English becomes the main or dominant language, it becomes convenient to use and the local language isn't used anymore.

  Bill: So, how many different languages are there?

6 Yuko: It says in the book that if you put all the languages in a long line from number 1 with the most speakers, Chinese, to number 6, 700 with the fewest, the middle language would have 5,500 speakers.

  Bill: That's incredible.

7 Yuko: The book also says that half of the spoken languages in the world might disappear in 100 years. Not only that, by the year 2300 we might all be speaking the same language!

What surprised you about this conversation?

There are 6,700 oral (spoken) languages.

95% of the world's languages have fewer than 1 million speakers.

51% of the world's languages have fewer than 10,000 speakers.

How many world languages are there?

Everybody has heard of the "Harry Potter" series of books. Global sales of the "Potter" books in English are over 300 million, a number only exceeded by the Bible, some people say.

Although English is a very important world language read by many, many millions of people every day, there are thousands of languages. How many different spoken, or oral, languages are there in the world? Try to guess. 50? 100? 250? The answer, amazingly, is 6,700 different languages being spoken somewhere in the world.

Chinese has the largest number of first language speakers. This is because of China's huge population. Hindi and Bengali (and other languages) are spoken in India. The median language, however, has only 5,500 speakers. What does this mean? Well, if all the different spoken languages were put into a long line with Chinese being number 1 with 1,300,000,000 speakers to language with number 6,700, with the fewest speakers, the middle language would have only 5,500 speakers. This is pretty amazing.

Papua New Guinea has 836 different languages and Indonesia has 707. In Africa, Nigeria has 517 different languages. Twelve languages have disappeared in Nigeria since the last edition of this book. Almost all countries have more than one language. Even Britain has three different spoken languages: English (of course), Welsh (spoken in Wales), and Gaelic which is spoken by a very small number of people in parts of Ireland and Scotland. The Cornish language has disappeared. Mr. Burden has a friend whose first language is Welsh.

Languages with the most first language speakers	
1) Chinese	1,300,000,000
2) Spanish	485,000,000
3) English	373,000,000
4) Arabic	362,000,000
5) Hindi	344,000,000
6) Bengali	234,000,000
7) Portuguese	232,000,000

Countries with the most different languages:	
1) Papua New Guinea	836
2) Indonesia	707
3) Nigeria	517
4) India	447
5) China	302
6) Mexico	287

Are you surprised by this? Here are some other interesting facts:

1) Europe and the Middle East together have only 4% (275) of the world's spoken languages.

2) North, South and Central America together have 15% (about 1,000) of the world's languages.

3) Africa has 30% (2,011) of the world's languages. Apparently, 171 of these languages will die out soon, or have already died out.

4) Asia has 32% (2,165) of the world's languages.

5) The Pacific region alone has 19% (1,302) different spoken languages.

World languages

Look at the sentences below and try to guess the missing numbers. Choose the numbers from below and write the numbers on the line. Cover the answers below!

1. _____ % of the World's population speaks Mandarin Chinese.

2. _____ languages are in danger of disappearing.

3. _____ % of Africans do not have education in their first language.

4. 96% of the World's population only speak _____ % of the world's languages.

5. 500 languages have fewer than _____ people who speak them.

6. Wikipedia has articles in _____ languages.

7. One language dies every _____ days.

8. There are _____ official working languages in the EU.

9. The UN has _____ official languages: Arabic, Chinese, English, French, Russian, and Spanish.

10. _____ % of Africans do not know the official language of their country.

a) 14   b) 2,400   c) 100   d) 90   e) 6   f) 250   g) 4   h) 24

i) 87   j) 12.44

1) 12.44% of the World's population speaks Mandarin Chinese.

2) 2,400 languages are in danger of disappearing.

3) 87% of Africans do not have education in their first language.

4) 96% of the World's population only speak 4% of the world's languages.

5) 500 languages have fewer than 100 people who speak them.

6) Wikipedia has articles in 250 languages.

7) One language dies every 14 days.

8) There are 24 official working languages in the EU.

9) The UN has 6 official languages: Arabic, Chinese, English, French, Russian, and Spanish.

10) 90% of Africans do not know the official language of their country.

Learning English

1. In my opinion, learning English is ____.
a) always interesting
b) usually interesting
c) sometimes interesting
d) usually not very interesting
e) never interesting
f) _____

2. I think that learning English will ___ get a good job.
a) definitely help me to
b) maybe help me to
c) maybe not help me to
d) definitely not help me to
e) _____

3. I think that English is ____.
a) the easiest foreign language
b) a pretty easy foreign language
c) sometimes a difficult foreign language
d) a very difficult foreign language

4. To become a good English speaker, we have to _____.
a) study for 2 hours everyday
b) study for 2 or 3 years
c) study for 3 to 5 years
d) study for ever
e) _____

5. In English class, when the teacher asks me a question I feel _____.
a) frightened
b) my heart pounding
c) sometimes afraid
d) pretty relaxed
e) happy
f) _____

6. When I hear the word "English", _____ comes to mind.
a) "it's difficult"
b) "I can't speak it"
c) "it's pretty easy"
d) "it's hard to understand"
e) "it's fun"
f) "it's a necessary evil"
g) _____

7. In English class, when I talk to my partner in English, I feel _____.
a) it is fun
b) relaxed
c) uncomfortable
d) Strange. Why am I speaking in English to a Japanese person?
e) a bit bored
f) _____

8. I sometimes wonder _____.
a) why am I here, today?
b) if I'm wasting my time
c) if I will ever be a good speaker
d) why other people in the class are so good at English?
e) if I will ever use English after I graduate
f) _____

9. I _____ think I would rather study something else instead of English.
a) always
b) usually   e) rarely
c) sometimes   f) never
d) occasionally   g) _____

10. I think that other students in this class are ____.
a) better than me at English
b) not as good as me
c) as good as me
d) as poor as me
e) of many different levels

11. I think I will _____ use English after I graduate.
a) definitely
b) probably
c) maybe
d) probably not

12. This is because _____

13. Outside of class, I _____.
a) never use English
b) talk to my friends in English
c) communicate in English on SNS
d) watch TV dramas in English
e) surf the Internet in English
f) _____

Opinions about learning foreign languages

Here are some opinions of Japanese people about foreign languages.

Answers in percent

How interested are Japanese people in mastering a foreign language	Male	Female
1) Very interested	___	32.1
2) Somewhat interested	30.4	22.6
3) Not really interested	19.6	17.6
4) Not at all interested	21.6	a

The degree of importance of English in society (regardless of ability)	Male	Female
1) Definitely	38.9	___
2) A little	40.2	51
3) Not at all	20.9	16.9

Whether English ability will improve after becoming compulsory in elementary school	
1) Not improve	c
2) improve a little	49
3) Improve a lot	1.9

What kind of study outside of school will be necessary to improve English	
1) Short term study abroad	52.8
2) Cram schools or conversation schools	43.2
3) DVDs	28
4) Computer software	21.5
5) Listening to CDs	21.2

Why English will become important	
1) To widen their sphere of communication	39.3
2) To increase job opportunities	31.5
3) To have a global way of thinking	e
4) To contribute to international society	4.2

Which language are people interested in	
1) English	87.3
2) Chinese	___
3) French	7.9
4) Korean	7
5) German	5.3

The degree of confidence in English	
1) Completely	2.3
2) A little	___
3) Not at all	79.3

Where people have spoken with foreigners in English	
1) Street	53.8
2) Station	38.7
3) Sightseeing spot	___
4) Shop	11.9
5) Airport	11

a) What percent of males are very interested in mastering a foreign language?

b) What percent of people are interested in learning Chinese?

c) What percent of females think English is definitely important?

d) What percent of people are a little confident in their English?

e) What percent of people have spoken to foreigners in English at a sightseeing spot?

f) What percent of people: _____

g) Now ask about a: _____

h) Now ask about c: _____

i) Now ask about e: _____

j) _____

k) _____

Opinions about learning foreign languages

Here are some opinions of Japanese people about foreign languages.

How interested are Japanese people in mastering a foreign language	Male	Female
1) Very interested	28.4	32.1
2) Somewhat interested	30.4	
3) Not really interested	19.6	b
4) Not at all interested	21.6	16.6

The degree of importance of English in society (regardless of ability)	Male	Female
1) Definitely	d	32.1
2) A little	40.2	51
3) Not at all	___	16.9

Whether English ability will improve after becoming compulsory in elementary school	
1) Not improve	49.1
2) improve a little	___
3) Improve a lot	1.9

What kind of study outside of school will be necessary to improve English	
1) Short term study abroad	f
2) Cram schools or conversation schools	43.2
3) DVDs	28
4) Computer software	21.5
5) Listening to CDs	21.2

Why English will become important	
1) To widen their sphere of communication	39.3
2) To increase job opportunities	___
3) To have a global way of thinking	12.3
4) To contribute to international society	4.2

Answers in percent

Which language are people interested in	
1) English	___
2) Chinese	9.6
3) French	7.9
4) Korean	7
5) German	5.3

The degree of confidence in English	
1) Completely	2.3
2) A little	18.4
3) Not at all	79.3

Where people have spoken with foreigners in English	
1) Street	53.8
2) Station	38.7
3) Sightseeing spot	21.5
4) Shop	11.9
5) Airport	11

a) What percent of females are somewhat interested in mastering a foreign language?

b) What percent of people are interested in learning English?

c) What percent of males think English is not at all important?

d) What percent of people think children's English ability will improve a little?

e) What percent of people think English will become important to increase their job chances?

f) What percent of people: _____

g) Now ask about b: _____

h) Now ask about d: _____

i) Now ask about f: _____

j) _____

k) _____

My beliefs about learning English

What are your beliefs about learning English?

Put a circle (○) in the correct box for your answer.

Then, ask your partner. Put a triangle (▽) in the correct box for his or her answer.

If you have a ○ and a ▽ in the same box, you have something in common.

Ask your partner: _____.What do you think?

	1	2	3	4	5
1. English is the most important world language					
2. Everyone must study English in high school					
3. Learning English is a waste of time					
4. I wish I could study other subjects, instead of English					
5. If you know English you can travel anywhere					
6. We don't need English because we can use AI like Chat GPT					
7. English is the language of the Internet					
8. Everyone must study English in elementary school					
9. If you don't know English, you can't get a good job					
10. Everyone should learn English until they speak it well					
11. Other foreign languages are equally important					
12. We shouldn't have to study English at university					
13. Chinese is becoming the most important foreign language					
14. We should only study English if we are interested in it					
15. I can't understand why we have to learn English					
16. Because of English, other languages are dying					
17. . . .					
18. . . .					
19. . . .					

1= No, I completely disagree with this idea
2= No, I partly disagree with this idea
3= I'm not sure I agree or disagree with this idea
4= Yes, I partly agree with this idea
5= Yes, I completely agree with this idea

What about you?

What do you think?

How about you?

We both completely disagree that *English is the most important foreign language.*

1) We both completely disagree that _____.

2) We both partly disagree that _____.

3) We both partly agree that _____.

4) We both completely agree that _____.

5) We both are not sure if _____.

My experiences of learning English

Write and tell me about some of your experiences of learning and studying English until now. Please write about:

1) When and where you started to learn English.
2) How you felt at that time.
3) Your English lessons in junior high school.
4) Your English lessons in senior high school.
5) What you would like to study or do in your English classes now.

1. *I started learning English*

2. *At that time I felt*

3. *In junior high school, I*

4. *In senior high school, I*

5. *In my English classes now, I would like*

Why learn English?

Many people have many opinions about learning English. Some of you may **resent** having to learn English.

After all, English is a **compulsory subject** at university. Some of you, however, may really like learning English.

What are your opinions? How about the opinions of your classmates? What do you have in common?

Ask three classmates some questions.

	YOUR answers:	Person 1 Name: _____	Person 2 Name: _____	Person 3 Name: _____
1) How do you feel before coming to this class on *(put in the day)* _____ ?				
2) What **did** you think of English classes in high school? Can you think of 3 words?	a) b) c)	a) b) c)	a) b) c)	a) b) c)
3) What **do** you think of English classes in university now? Can you think of 3 words?	a) b) c)	a) b) c)	a) b) c)	a) b) c)
4) Do you think that studying English is important? Why or why not?				
5) Which do you think is more important "conversation" or "grammar and reading" classes? Why?	Why:	Why:	Why:	Why:
6) What would you like to do more of in this class?				
7) Do you think you will continue studying English after you graduate?				

What do you have in common?

Mr/Miss _____ and I think _____ .

Mr/Miss _____ and I think _____ .

Mr/Miss _____ and I think _____ .

UNIT

8

My beliefs

Bill and Yuko are chatting about things they believe in. Before you read, find the answers to these questions:

1) *What has Yuko been reading about recently?*
2) *What kind of dream did Bill have? What did he do after?*
3) *What does Yuko say is pretty popular in Japan?*
4) *What podcast did Bill listen to recently?*

Now, read the conversation with your partner:

¹ Yuko: You know, I've been reading this book about blood types...

　Bill:　 Oh, I know. You mean how you can tell people's character by their blood types...

² Yuko: Yeah, it's great. I really think it's true. It certainly matches my type.

　Bill:　 Oh, come on! You can't be serious. That's not true, is it? You'll be telling me next you read books about dreams, too.

³ Yuko: Well, I used to. I believe you can learn a lot by analysing your dreams.

　Bill:　 I'm not so sure. Someone did tell me that if you dream of a white snake you will become rich...

⁴ Yuko: I've heard that too.

　Bill:　 Anyway, I did see a snake in a dream and so I bought a lottery ticket. And guess what?

⁵ Yuko: What? You won a lot of money?

　Bill:　 Yeah, my numbers did come up. But, unfortunately, I only won 2,000 yen.

⁶ Yuko: That's too bad. Have you ever tried *uranai*? This is pretty popular in Japan, too. I've had my fortune told once or twice.

　Bill:　 You really believe in that stuff? You'll be telling me you believe in crystal balls next!

⁷ Yuko: So what do you believe in?

　Bill:　 Well actually, I heard a strange story the other day and it seems unbelievable, but true. I was listening to a podcast which said that the chances of Earth being hit by a big meteorite is really high....

⁸ Yuko: Really? What else did the podcast say?

　Bill:　 It said that most scientists are keeping their fingers crossed!

How about you? Do you share any of these beliefs? Ask your partner:

1) Do you believe you can tell a person's character from their blood type?
2) Do you believe that dreams have meanings?
3) Have you ever tried *uranai*?
4) Do you think that one day Earth will be struck by a large meteorite?

70

Blood types

Some people say that you can know a person's character by their blood type. For example, if you are shy or nervous, your blood type could be 'A' type. Do you think this is maybe true?

1. I think you can _____ know a person's character by their blood type.
a) definitely
b) probably
c) maybe
d) probably not
e) definitely not
f) _____

2. I think the craze of buying books about blood types is _____ .
a) something I'm not interested in at all
b) something I am very interested in
c) a waste of money
d) something I may be interested in
e) _____

3. Before I decide to get married, I would ____ to know my partner's blood type.
a) definitely like
b) be somewhat interested
c) be a little curious
d) not be interested at all
e) _____

4. I _____ my blood type and the blood type of my close friends.
a) of course know
b) have no idea about
c) _____

5. If I could change my blood type, I would
_____ .
a) like to be A type
b) like to be AB type
c) like to be O type
d) like to be B type
e) have no interest in changing
f) _____

6. My best friend and I have _____.
a) the same blood type
b) a different blood type
c) maybe the same type, but I've never asked.

7. I think _____ be friends with people who have a different blood type from me.
a) I can't
b) I can easily
c) it would be difficult to
d) _____

8. I think that employers should _____ staff by their blood type.
a) definitely choose
b) definitely not choose
c) maybe choose
d) maybe not choose
e) _____

9. If I joined a DVD rental shop and the form asked about blood type, I would feel _____.
a) that I don't care
b) that it is a little strange
c) that it is a good idea
d) that such information is private
e) that it is ridiculous
f) _____

10. I think that my blood type _____ my personality.
a) definitely matches
b) somewhat matches
c) doesn't at all match
d) matches a little with

11. I think that believing in star signs and fortune telling is _____.
a) very useful
b) a load of rubbish
c) sometimes a good idea
d) very helpful for me
e) something that may be true
f) _____

12. I believe in:
_____

Common dreams: What do our dreams signify?

Teacher (s)

To see a teacher (past or present) in your dream, suggests that you are looking for some advice, guidance, or knowledge. You are heading into a new path in life and ready to learn from a past experience.

Teeth

To dream that you have rotten teeth, warns that your health and/or business is in trouble. You may have said some bad words and those words are coming back to haunt you. To dream that your teeth are gleaming, signifies happiness and fulfilled wishes, while a tooth falling out which you try to hide suggests a lack of confidence. Brushing your teeth can mean you are not aggressive enough and you need to be careful about yourself and your own interest.

Snakes

To see a snake or be bitten by one in your dream signifies some hidden fears and worries that are threatening you. Your dream may be alerting you to something in your waking life that you are not aware of or that has not yet surfaced. However, seeing a white snake in your dreams may be lucky for your future!

Cats

To see a cat in your dream, symbolizes an independent spirit, creativity, and power. It can also represent misfortune and bad luck.

Driving

To dream that you are driving a car signifies your life's journey and your path in life. The dream is telling of how you are moving and navigating through life. If you are driving and cannot see the road ahead of you, then it indicates that you do not know where you are headed in life and what you really want to do with yourself. You are lacking direction and goals. If you are driving on a curvy road, this indicates that you are having difficulties in achieving your goals.

"I'm Naked!" (But ONLY you!)

In your dream you are going about your normal routine - going to work, waiting for the bus, or just walking down the street - when you suddenly realize that you are completely naked! Dreaming that you are naked is very common. Nudity symbolizes a variety of things depending on your real life situation. Realizing that you are naked in public reflects your vulnerability or feelings of shamefulness. You may be hiding something and are afraid that others can see right through you.

Now can you take it in turns and explain in your own words what these dreams signify:
a) Teachers If you dream about teachers this means _____
b) Teeth _____
c) Snakes _____
d) Cats _____
e) Driving _____
f) Being naked _____

My beliefs

What are your beliefs? Here are some questions. Ask your partner.

Put a circle (○) in the correct box for your answer.

Then, ask your partner. Put a triangle (▽) in the correct box for his or her answer.

If you have a ○ and a ▽ in the same box, you have something in common.

Do you believe that...	1	2	3	4	5
1. we can tell a lot about a person from their blood types?					
2. our dreams can give us useful information?					
3. there are such things as ghosts or vampires?					
4. carrying lucky charms bring good luck?					
5. palm reading can give us a good idea about our future?					
6. it is important to know our star sign?					
7. there is life after we die?					
8. there is life somewhere on another planet?					
9. one day Earth will be hit by a large meteorite?					
10. you should read your daily horoscope in the newspaper?					
11. there is such a thing as magic?					
12. seeing the same dream a number of times is a warning?					
13. cutting your fingernails at night brings bad luck?					
14. you shouldn't sleep with your head facing north?					
15. . . .(your idea)					
16. . . .(your idea)					
17. . . .(your idea)					

1= No, I believe this is completely untrue
2= No, this is probably untrue
3= Maybe this is true. I haven't thought about it much
4= Yes, this is probably true
5= Yes, I believe this is completely true

What about you?

What do you think?

How about you?

Anything in common?

1) We both think it is completely untrue that *UFOS have probably landed somewhere on Earth* .

1) We both think it is completely untrue that _____.

2) We both think it is probably untrue that _____.

3) We both think that maybe it is true that _____.

4) We both think it is probably true that _____.

5) We both think it is completely true that _____.

Common Superstitions

Here are some common superstitions from around the World. Let's read them. Do you believe that they are true?

Japan:

- If you cut your nails at night, you will not be able to see your parents before they die, or alternatively, you will die early.
- When you see a funeral car, hide your thumbs or a family member will die soon.
- When you buy new shoes, make sure to only wear them in the morning.
- Don't sleep with your head pointing north. This is the way that dead people are laid to rest at a funeral.
- If you buy a wallet in the Fall, you will not become a rich person. But buying a wallet in the New Year is lucky.

China:

- A home numbered 8, or a number 8 on a license plate or a hotel room will bring good luck.
- During the Chinese New Year, scissors, knives and any other sharp instruments are to be stored away to avoid good luck from being cut off.
- At New Year, as in other countries, wearing red brings good luck.

Other countries:

- Couples like to give each other another a present or gift to show their love. In the Philippines, there is a belief that one should avoid giving handkerchiefs as a gift. This is because a handkerchief is usually associated with crying or sad moments.
- In Ireland, there is a belief that to protect a child during birth, one should put a knife on the doorstep to stop bad or evil spirits entering their house. Evil spirits cannot cross the iron or steal the knife to do any harm to the baby.
- In Venezuela, there is a tradition for women to wear yellow clothes on New Year's Day. If they do, they believe that they will be lucky all year around.

Other common superstitions:

- Friday the thirteenth is an unlucky day.
- A rabbit's foot brings good luck.
- If you walk under a ladder, you will have bad luck.
- If a black cat crosses your path you will have bad luck.
- We should cross our fingers or touch something wooden for good luck.

Does your blood type match your personality?

Here are some characteristics of blood types. Try to guess your partner's blood type by asking him or her questions. For example: "Are you shy?"

A TYPE		B TYPE	
optimistic	quiet	practical	patient
nervous	secretive	optimistic	untidy
serious	stubborn	selfish	impulsive
kind	shy	independent	hardworking
low self-confidence		friendly	tight fisted
persistent		easily embarrassed	
O TYPE		AB TYPE	
romantic	childish moody	cheerful	likes peace
kind	talkative	intelligent	likes harmony
friendly	likes risks	emotional	likes games
stubborn	persistent	sometimes impolite	
generous	often worries	closed- minded	

After asking my partner some questions, I think my partner's blood type is _____.

Actually, his or her blood type is _____.

I think that asking questions about blood type is _____.

Do you think these characteristics are true? Do they match YOUR blood type?

_____.

I think my teacher's blood type is _____.

Complete these sentences about your character:

I think that my character is _____.

I would like to be more _____.

One thing I don't like about my character is _____.

Sometimes I wish that I were _____.

Ask your partner

Here are many questions. Choose about TEN that look interesting to you.

Ask and answer questions. When you answer, say "How about you?" or "What do you think?"

Ask your partner...	Ask your partner...	Ask your partner...	Ask your partner...
Do you believe in UFOs? Answer:	Do you carry anything for good luck? Answer:	Is it unlucky to swim in the sea during *O-bon*? Answer:	What are you afraid of? Answer:
Do you ever hide your thumbs? Answer:	Are you worried that our planet will be hit by meteorites? Answer:	Do you think seeing a spider is unlucky? Answer:	Do you believe that opening an umbrella inside will bring bad luck? Answer:
Do you believe that walking under ladders is unlucky? Answer:	Do you believe in life after death? Answer:	Do you believe the number 4 is unlucky? Answer:	What did your mother use to tell you to stop bad luck? Answer:
Do you believe that breaking a mirror will bring bad luck? Answer:	What do you do for good luck? Answer:	Did you use to hide your belly button during thunder? Answer:	Do (or did) you believe in horoscopes? Answer:
Ask your partner... Answer:	Ask your partner... Answer:	Ask your partner... Answer:	Ask your partner... Answer:

Do you and your partner have any beliefs that are the same, now or when you were a kid?

We both believe that _____.

We both used to believe that _____.

Do you and your partner have any beliefs that are different?

My partner believes _____, but I _____.

Ask your partner

Here are many questions. Choose about TEN that look interesting to you.

Ask and answer questions. When you answer, say "How about you?" or "What do you think?"

Ask your partner...	Ask your partner...	Ask your partner...	Ask your partner...
Do you believe in ghosts? Answer:	Is it OK to sleep facing north? Answer:	Do you believe in fortune telling? Answer:	Can you tell a person's character by their blood type? Answer:
Do you cross your fingers for good luck? Answer:	Do you cut your nails at night? Answer:	Do you believe there is life on a different planet? Answer:	Did you use to throw beans on *Setsubun?* Answer:
Did you do anything for good luck as a kid? Answer:	What did your mother use to tell you for good luck? Answer:	Did you use to believe in Santa Claus? Answer:	Do you ever touch wood for good luck? Answer:
Do you believe in *uranai*? Answer:	Do you carry anything to stop bad luck? Answer:	Is it OK to wear new shoes in the evening? Answer:	Do you believe the number 8 is lucky? Answer:
Ask your partner... Answer:	Ask your partner... Answer:	Ask your partner... Answer:	Ask your partner... Answer:

Do you and your partner have any beliefs that are the same, now or when you were a kid?

We both believe that _____.

We both used to believe that _____.

Do you and your partner have any beliefs that are different?

My partner believes _____, but I _____.

B

My dreams and superstitions

Write and tell me about some of your dreams and superstitions. Please write about:

1) A dream that you had recently.

2) A superstition that someone taught you when you were a child.

3) Something that you believe in.

4) Your experiences of fortune telling (Horoscopes, star signs, palm reading, *uranai*).

1. *A dream that I had recently was*

2. *When I was a kid, I was taught that*

3. *These days, I believe in*

4. *In my experience fortune telling is*

UNIT 9

The future

Bill's year in Japan is nearly at an end. He is going back home soon.

First, find the answers to these questions:

1) *What is Bill's future goal?*

2) *What does Yuko want to do in the near future?*

3) *What is Bill's burning ambition?*

4) *What does Yuko hope to do one day?*

Now, read the conversation with a partner:

1 Yuko: So, Bill. Your year in Japan is nearly over.

Bill: That's right. As people say: **"Time flies like an arrow."**

2 Yuko: Well, have you had fun?

Bill: Yes, of course. It's been great. I have many good memories.

3 Yuko: So, what are your plans in back in England?

Bill: Well, I have to study Japanese hard so I can get a good job after I graduate, of course.

4 Yuko: What's your **future goal**?

Bill: If I become better at speaking and reading, I want to become a translator. My **aim** is to get a job using Japanese language. Maybe in tourism.

5 Yuko: Good luck!

Bill: How about you? What are some of your **future plans**?

6 Yuko: I want to get my teaching license and become an English teacher. In the **near future**, I'd like to brush up my English doing a homestay.

Bill: **In the next year or two**, I'd like to come back to Japan. Maybe I could work at a *ryokan* in the summer season.

7 Yuko: Do you have any **burning ambitions**?

Bill: Well, one day I'd like to travel more in Asia. **If I have the chance**, I'd like to visit Angkor Wat in Cambodia, and then see the Great Wall in China. There are so many places I want to go! So many different kinds of food to eat!

8 Yuko: Sounds great! **I'd really like to** take a long trip to South America to visit Macchu Picchu in Peru, **one day**.

Bill: Wow, that sounds great! It's important to have aims in life!

9 Yuko: Yeah, maybe I could see you soon if I do that homestay in England!

Bill: That's a great plan!

How about you? Ask your partner about their future plans, aims in life and burning ambitions.

79

In the future

1. I am _____ about my future.
a) optimistic
b) a little worried
c) very worried
d) not thinking
e) relaxed
f) a little pessimistic
g) _____

2. Thinking about my own future, now I
   am _____.
a) very excited
b) so nervous I just want to forget it
c) looking forward to whatever happens
d) just hoping everything will be OK
e) thinking it will be great
f) _____

3. After I graduate, I think it will be __ to get a
   good job.
a) pretty easy
b) pretty difficult
c) very easy
d) very difficult
e) impossible
f) _____

4. Sometime in the future, I _____ live, work, or
   study in a foreign country.
a) really want to
b) will definitely
c) am not going to
d) don't think I'll

5. When I am 50 years old, I will
   _____ be studying English!
a) definitely still
b) definitely not
c) perhaps still
d) probably still

6. When I am 40, I think I will _____.
a) drive an expensive, foreign car
b) be a successful businessperson
c) be living in a house I bought
d) be in prison
e) _____

7. When I am 50, I think I will ___.
a) be happily married with two kids
b) be rich and famous
c) be the owner of my company
d) be rich and gambling in Las Vegas
e) _____

8. When I am 30, my hobby will be _____.
a) playing golf
b) singing karaoke with my old classmates
c) spending time with my kids
d) spending time outdoors hiking and cycling
e) _____

9. 40 years from now, I will _____.
a) be wearing a wig
b) have no hair!
c) be listening to the same music as now
d) look about the same as today
e) wear a hearing aid
f) _____

10. Something on my 'bucket list' is _____.
a) traveling around Japan by *Honda Cub*
b) scuba diving in Australia or Okinawa
c) bungee jumping in New Zealand
d) trekking in the Himalayas
e) a safari in Africa
f) _____

11. The main thing that worries me about the fu-
    ture of this planet is that _____.
a) global warming will be a big problem
b) the world's supply of oil will run out
c) there won't be enough food for everyone
d) there will be another major war
e) the big cities will be very polluted
f) _____

12. When I think about the distant future of the
    world, I am _____.
a) very worried
b) a little worried
c) pessimistic
d) optimistic
e) quite cheerful
f) _____

13. In the future, people in Japan will ___.
a) be happier than now
b) be less happy than now
c) be richer than now
d) be poorer than now
e) _____

14. A future, burning ambition of mine is to
    _____ .

Try to predict your partner's future.

First, guess. Then, ask questions like this: "So, which prefecture do you think you will live in, when you're 40?"

At 40

At 40…	Your guess	Your partner's answer	right or wrong
What prefecture will your partner live in?			
What job will he/she be doing?			
Will your partner be married?			
How many kids will he/she have?			
What kind of car will he/she drive?			
What will his/her hairstyle be like?			
Where will his/her honeymoon have been?			
What will his/her interests be?			
_____ ?			
_____ ?			

I'm only guessing but perhaps…

I have no idea, but maybe…

The Future

Here are some topics about the future. Discuss them with a partner. Use phrases like these:

"One day in the future, I'd like to _____."

"If I have the chance, I'd really like to _____."

1. A trip somewhere not in Japan	2. An interesting trip in Japan	3. Place to live
4. A future possession	5. Home	6. My family
7. My appearance	8. Freetime	9. A challenge
10. An adventure	11. Sport or fitness activity	12. My car
13.	14.	15.

Did you find anything in common about your future?

My partner and I both _____.

Long term ambitions

Now find out what some long term ambitions your classmates and your teacher hold.

Ask questions beginning like this: "What are your ambitions or hopes *in the next long vacation* ?"

	Teacher:	Me:	Person 1:	Person 2:	Person 3:
in the next long vacation					
in the next year or two					
in the next three years or so (after you graduate)					
in the next ten years					
in the distant future					

What do you have in common?

Mr/Miss and I _____ will maybe _____ .

Mr/Miss and I _____ will maybe _____ .

Mr/Miss and I _____ will maybe _____ .

Ask your partner

Ask your partner these questions. When you answer your partner's questions, use:

Yes, definitely   *Yes, possibly*   *No, it's not likely (but)*

Yes, it's likely   *Yes, maybe*   *No, definitely not*   How about you?

Ask your partner...	Ask your partner...	Ask your partner...	Ask your partner...
Do you think the World's oil will run out? Answer:	Will you be happily married with two kids in the future? Answer:	Do you think you will ever visit the North Pole? Answer:	Do you think there will be a third World War? Answer:
Ask your partner... Do you think China will be the richest country, someday? Answer:	Ask your partner... Will there be cheap flights to the Moon, someday? Answer:	Ask your partner... Do you think life on another planet will be found? Answer:	Ask your partner... Do you think your hobby at 40 will be golf? Answer:
Ask your partner... Do you think you will ever live abroad? Answer:	Ask your partner... Will you be rich and famous, someday? Answer:	Ask your partner... Do you think you will visit the Taj Mahal, someday? Answer:	Ask your partner... Do you think Japan can win the soccer World Cup? Answer:
Ask your partner... Will people be happier in the future? Answer:	Ask your partner... Do you think you will wear a wig in the future? Answer:	Ask your partner... Will you win big money on the lottery one day? Answer:	Ask your partner... Do you think you will ever try sky diving? Answer:
Ask your partner... Answer:	Ask your partner... Answer:	Ask your partner... Answer:	Ask your partner... Answer:

What do you and your partner have in common?

We both think that _____.

What do you and your partner disagree about?

My partner thinks that _____ but I think _____.

A

Ask your partner

Ask your partner these questions. When you answer your partner's questions, use:

Yes, definitely   *Yes, possibly*   *No, it's not likely (but)*

Yes, it's likely   *Yes, maybe*   *No, definitely not*

> How about you?

Ask your partner... Will people live on the Moon, someday? Answer:	Ask your partner... Do you think Japan will ever have a woman Prime Minister? Answer:	Ask your partner... Can people live to 150 years old in the future? Answer:	Ask your partner... Do you think you will ever try bungee jumping? Answer:
Ask your partner... Can the Hanshin Tigers win the Japan series soon? Answer:	Ask your partner... Do you think you will be married before you are 30? Answer:	Ask your partner... Do you think you will visit the Galapagos Islands? Answer:	Ask your partner... Will you be living in Hokkaido or Okinawa in the future? Answer:
Ask your partner... Do you think everyone will drive electric cars one day? Answer:	Ask your partner... Do you think you will ever drive around Japan by Honda Cub? Answer:	Ask your partner... Can you be an excellent speaker of English someday? Answer:	Ask your partner... Is there a chance you will own a foreign car at 40? Answer:
Ask your partner... Do you think your honeymoon will be in Hawaii? Answer:	Ask your partner... Will you be living in Okayama 10 years later? Answer:	Ask your partner... Will you still be learning English at 40? Answer:	Ask your partner... Do you think you will ever visit the Pyramids? Answer:
Ask your partner... Answer:	Ask your partner... Answer:	Ask your partner... Answer:	Ask your partner... Answer:

What do you and your partner have in common?

We both think that _____.

What do you and your partner disagree about?

My partner thinks that _____ but I think _____.

B

In the future

Write and tell me about something about your hopes and ambitions for the future. Please write about:

1) Your life after you graduate.

2) What you will be doing twenty years from now.

3) Things you want to achieve.

4) Your hometown in fifty years.

1. *After I graduate,*

2. *Twenty years later, I think I will be*

3. *In the future, there are many things I want to achieve. First,*

4. *Fifty years from now, my hometown will be*

THINK OF 6 INTERESTING QUESTIONS:

Ask three people. Do NOT ask the person sitting next to you!

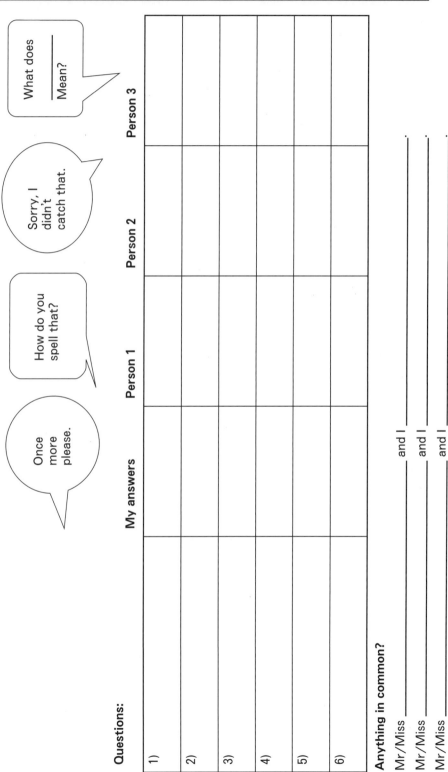

Once more please.

How do you spell that?

Sorry, I didn't catch that.

What does _____ Mean?

Theme:

Questions:	My answers	Person 1	Person 2	Person 3
1)				
2)				
3)				
4)				
5)				
6)				

Anything in common?

Mr/Miss _____ and I _____.

Mr/Miss _____ and I _____.

Mr/Miss _____ and I _____.

THINK OF 6 INTERESTING QUESTIONS:

Ask three people. Do NOT ask the person sitting next to you!

Questions:

Theme:			
My answers	Person 1	Person 2	Person 3
1)			
2)			
3)			
4)			
5)			
6)			

Once more please.

How do you spell that?

Sorry, I didn't catch that.

What does ____ Mean?

Anything in common?

Mr/Miss _____ and I _____.

Mr/Miss _____ and I _____.

Mr/Miss _____ and I _____.

THINK OF 6 INTERESTING QUESTIONS:

Ask three people. Do NOT ask the person sitting next to you!

Theme:

Once more please.

How do you spell that?

Sorry, I didn't catch that.

What does ___ Mean?

Questions:

	My answers	Person 1	Person 2	Person 3
1)				
2)				
3)				
4)				
5)				
6)				

Anything in common?

Mr/Miss _____ and I _____ .

Mr/Miss _____ and I _____ .

Mr/Miss _____ and I _____ .

THINK OF 6 INTERESTING QUESTIONS:

Ask three people. Do NOT ask the person sitting next to you!

Once more please.

How do you spell that?

Sorry, I didn't catch that.

What does ——— Mean?

Questions:

	My answers	Person 1	Person 2	Person 3
1)				
2)				
3)				
4)				
5)				
6)				

Anything in common?

Mr/Miss _____ and I _____ .

Mr/Miss _____ and I _____ .

Mr/Miss _____ and I _____ .

■著者紹介

ピーター・バーデン（Peter Burden）

英国エクセター大学院教育学研究科（TESL：第二言語（英語）教授法）博士
（教育学博士 Doctor of Education Ed.D）

岡山商科大学教授

Intermediate
Let's have a natter 〔中級〕 英語の世間話 第4版
－small talk in the classroom－

2015 年 9 月 20 日　第 3 版第 1 刷発行
2023 年 8 月 30 日　第 4 版第 1 刷発行

■著　　者───ピーター・バーデン
■発 行 者───佐藤　守
■発 行 所───株式会社 **大学教育出版**
　　　　　　　〒 700-0953 岡山市南区西市 855-4
　　　　　　　電話（086）244-1268　FAX（086）246-0294
■印刷製本───サンコー印刷 ㈱

ISBN978－4－86692－267－6